LIAR

LIAR

Lynn Crosbie

ANANSI

Published in 2006 by
House of Anansi Press Inc.
110 Spadina Avenue, Suite 801
Toronto, ON, M5V 2K4
Tel. 416-363-4343
Fax 416-363-1017
www.anansi.ca

Distributed in Canada by
HarperCollins Canada Ltd.
1995 Markham Road
Scarborough, ON, M1B 5M8
Toll free tel. 1-800-387-011

09 08 07 06   1 2 3 4 5

LIBRARY AND ARCHIVES CANADA CATALOGUING IN PUBLICATION DATA

Crosbie, Lynn, 1963–
Liar : a poem / Lynn Crosbie.
ISBN 0-88784-745-5
I. Title.
PS8555.R61166L52 2006   C811'.54   C2005-907346-2

Library of Congress Control Number: 2005939081

Cover design: Bill Douglas at The Bang
Text design and typesetting: Ingrid Paulson

*We acknowledge for their financial support of our publishing program the
Canada Council for the Arts, the Ontario Arts Council, and the Government of Canada
through the Book Publishing Industry Development Program (BPIDP).*

Printed and bound in Canada

For Mary

"You're in suspension. You're a liar. You're a liar a liar a liar / You lie."

—The Sex Pistols

"Secrets, silent, stony sit in the dark palaces of both our hearts: secrets weary of
their tyranny: tyrants willing to be dethroned."

— James Joyce

In the summer, your mother's cucumbers
in the bayou of her backyard, sunning themselves and snapping at the grass,
cater-corner to the lawn gnomes, boxes of pansies, gauntlets of marigold.

Arriving in fall, shrunken in brine, and forced behind the milk and cheese,
diminished and ghastly green, swaying

in some awful memory of what it is to be possessed of one's self, entirely.

That night I collected her freezer bags of cubed meat and tubby margarine
containers housing orange mush, fiddleheads, larded gravy.

Called you and left, as a message, the sound of the jar sailing over the hedges
and crashing.

In the morning, when I picked up the shards of glass, thinking of pigeons
stupidly pecking at the glitter,

the pickles had vanished. On stout angry legs, briny and furious,
they marched,

aching with the indignity, the affront—your mother's capable hands reaching out
and snapping them at the source.

Your parents dropped you off to take away more of your things,
and I asked, Did you tell them?

You nodded, and I raced out the door, banged on their car.

I suppose this is goodbye, I said, as your father cracked the window an inch or so.

I just wanted to say that—

They barked at me, Take care, and drove away so fast they scarred the road.

It is almost two years now.

I hear cars ignite and I think of them, taking the corner as I stood on our street,
one hand extended,

as it always was, in fear and uneasy love.

Your brother's self-portrait hung in our hallway for seven years. Its title cryptic,
something to do with private offenses that did and did not involve us.

In it, he holds his hand over his mouth.

His wife Debbie had an affair with a big shot at the company where they worked.
I never liked her.

When he learned the truth he came to you, he came to me and rested his head
on my shoulder, cried.

I never liked her, I said.

The company man would pass him in traffic and sneer.

He is fragile and ill, paints in egg tempera—reproductions of Flemish paintings
your parents hang by the decorative plates adorned with puppies of many breeds.

I have heard nothing from him since you left.

I feel his head, trying against me, and wonder at his tenderness, consider all the times he will reach for certainty and fail:

the deformed hand of the Frans Hals painting, dominating the entire canvas, the puppies, the contours of that disconsolate room.

We never had an anniversary, it was too difficult to calibrate.

The first time you cheated on your girlfriend, with me; the first of many times we would visit the sordid hotels you liked,

rife with vermin, the walls streaked with blood, the sound of screaming in the hallway, men smashing telephones down, cursing this bitch or that.

Infinite variations on the theme of sexual misconduct. You were so wild then, you once said to me.

I didn't care who I hurt, I was wild for you, which is what you meant and what I mean when I say I am ashamed.

The first time we met you were crashing my friend's wake.

You swept into the bar in a motley of scarves, your long hair tumbling, a cluster of black grapes.

You had met my friend briefly; still, we were aghast.

Imagine a murder of crows passing through a stone deity; imagine confetti commissioning the heads of prone invalids,

thrown from your graceful hands; you shook our hands and introduced yourself.
My friend was a trouble-maker who thrived on dissent.

I would wonder for years if he rigged this moment—
through the scrim of our tears, your gaudy arrival,

all the tears that would accumulate, unfallen, in the years to come.

You loved poetry, which is why you came—you decorated your body with
words and images, wrested from the untimely dead.

I see myself talking to the daughter I never had: Do not fall in love with poets.

They are always in love, Robert Lowell said.

To this I would add, Many of them will maintain, eventually, that it is not a lie,
but a metaphor.

For example, I killed the daughter I never had.

A girlfriend of mine was crying and you homed in on her,
patting her back, There, there.

You moved in with her two weeks later: you had a distinctive voice.

Low and larded with innuendo, lulling and sweet.

I think of this, remembering you wrapped around her.

I think of her shoulders heaving, her body's rigours.
A quiet drone surrounding her—

blowflies moiling among the dampness, the recesses of her sorrow.
Soon, you turned to me, as you would, for over seven years,
solemn and watchful.

As my own miseries pitched me into bed, deep into the filthy
nimbus of blankets and pillows,

you at the black post,
offering tea and handfuls of paper towels; I would refuse them,
and you would pad, quietly, away.

My place? Well, my bedroom is decorated in reds and oranges—

You wrote this in a letter to one of your girlfriends.

My bedroom, you said.

The red and the orange, my own attempt to be romantic, a spray of autumn
flowers, of autumn leaves,

the leaves that assemble late this fall, spoiled and glossy with decay.

In my own bedroom, the red drapes drawn. Pallid now, but still romantic:
how blood passes within us, its lividity disclosed,

how it passes, in blue conduits, like a lie that is easily detected,
like the rush of days uncounted, before you look out and see the fall.

It begins in flight—

You tear after me, through the corridors of Wilson Station, sit beside me on the bus
looking surprised and winded.

You run past the hedges hemming in the Lick'n Chicken, and burst in, joining me
at my table.

You had seen me blocks away—I look at mock-ups for your first book: on the cover,
there is a photograph your brother took. You look like Jesus, and it is disconcerting.

Last month I ran into one of your old friends who painted you this way.
Oh yes, the degenerate Christ, he said.

You race me to my door and grab me, suddenly, awfully; you say,
I will always love you.

When I graduated, you met me by the examination room,
with an armful of presents I would later forget in the taxi.

You told me you had put $500 in the card I had not opened;
replaced the other gifts.

I asked my parents what they thought of you, and they
liked that you had given me this,

and they were angry at you that it was lost.

If I had known how this incident would come to define us,
I would have robbed a bank,

or taken the driver out for a dinner of lobster and Pouilly Fuissé.

At this moment, and in my ignorance,
we were cut like cookies,

missing one integral ingredient, occasionally spilling over
with another,

the way that intentions spoil or exceed themselves:
the card should have been empty, you should have lied.

Your favourite movie is *The Unforgiven*:
some days, I feel like a slow-witted outlaw,

stumping through the sage.

Bullets ricochet off rocks and I notice the ledge
where you lie,

untroubled by taking away everything I have and will be.

Taking it away with Two Guys and a Van.

We watch this movie many times, and I never apprehend your passion—
locked away, loaded with everything you want and cannot have.

Silver homicides, executed with monstrous integrity.

I moved from our street a year after you left,
where you had edged me between your new apartment—

floreated window panes: in your bedroom, an approximation of orange
and red—

and your other girlfriend's place. Her address begins with one, and is otherwise
the same as mine.

When I walked our dog past, he would balk and plant his ass on the sidewalk.
I had not known:

You must have brought him there before.

My bedroom, dog—

He acted as though the street was suddenly filled with litter.

As though someone was waiting there to give him a needle, an open-handed slap.
What's wrong with you, I would say, chastising him.

I think of her in an acetate robe, offering him slices of Velveeta,
absent-mindedly, as you let his leash drag behind him.

Of one of your boasts: I am an incredible liar.

When I spoke to your best friend he was incredulous: he wouldn't do those things.
I know him.

Dogs are only aware of one thing.

I told your friend we seemed to be talking about two different people,

and my dog split the difference, between the path you took
and mine,

in the second instance, bullish with untaught loyalty.

What is lost is largely ineffable:

The fat boy with no eyes
A sock monkey named Lulu
Billy Bakers, a child who declared he was a close and personal friend of the cast of *Alien*
Legions of children with bat wings and Columbian accents
The small sailor who yelled about the starboard into your sleep
An old blind man who referred to you as Mother and others,

What we created together; dissembling—
how this vanished into thin air.

I am yelling at you and you run upstairs, hurl yourself on the bed,
roll into a ball and cry.

I feel remorse, assure you that whoever hurt you in the past
will not hurt you again.

Toward the end, when you touch me and I cringe, when I fall in love
with this man or that man,

I think of what I think of as your beautiful face,
disfigured with tears,

and know that I can never betray you.

I Spy listing:

> — College streetcar, rush hour, dark hair,
>   eyes, we talked about Stendhal, shall we
>   continue our conversation?

This was you, hanging off the bar like an ape,
scarlet mouth; your eyes, Glossettes.

My heart in my throat, tearing it out then tossing it,

how it fit into me like a tire nailed to a tree
between two others,

and then some.
Spinoza fitting logic into pieces,

falling in love,

transporting wildlife in boxcars—the usual mayhem,
banana skins and puke,

the unusual sound of different predators,
their teeth bared as they calculate the distance

between seizures, other obstructions.

Your face is beautiful—I am reminded of this constantly. Friends and strangers
seem incredulous.

Your pale face, masses of jet hair, eyes,
the body of a frangible saint.

You seem oblivious to this, seeking out homely friends and lovers,
who round you out, who surround you like white tissue,

like clods of earth.

It is the kind of beauty that causes injury:

Like our brief love affair with narcotics—cutting through clean
little drifts.

And later, after you,

upending drawers for a phone number, walking the streets in pyjamas to find an ATM,
razoring each of my jewel cases for a line,

I would remember you as an 8-ball, about to be delivered,
quivering in its glassine bag,

stamped with aces of spades: what I want and what I hate.

Sweetness—the names we called each other, asinine,
astronomical then, in the reach and the miss,

you called me Angel.

I have not saved the letters, but remember the flourish of this address,
remember occupying the name,

in my own dreadful way.

Among your files I would find letters to old lovers, casual friends,
addressed the same way.

Everyone is an angel the day they die.

This week, I have finished throwing out everything your mother ever gave me—

left the crystal vase on the street and a woman in veils stopped and hefted it,
suspicious. It's bad luck for me, I told her, change it—

Pitched the vacuum that smouldered and burned its contents,
broke the cookie jar, by accident.

The Beanie Babies are still boxed at my parent's house:
limpid animals, with birth-date tags and names like Cheezer, Blessed, and Schnitzel.

She began collecting them and it soon became an obsession. Your brother bought her
a wooden hanging tree,

I began scouring mini-malls for giraffes, beavers, ponies, teddy bears of various countries.

I would stack them in boxes and send them to her; on our rare visits, arrive
with bags of plush bounty.

Her face softening—

I began collecting them myself. Hiding them in a box, unsure of their appeal,
slightly repelled: I have never liked to hold such things.

The obsession faded out: the pumpkin, four-leaf-clovered and Santa babies listing on the tree,

the shelves in your old room still groaning with her strange zoo, emanating neglect. It is hard to surrender passion, of any kind.

Prior to this, the room was filled with your high-school trophies, a one-side-finished Rubik's Cube.

The weight of expectations and regret: shifting, unstable.

My own trepidation, as someone without children, also—

at the idea of nurturing something soft and malleable,
your apprehension ultimately exceeding your desire.

We would wait in the basement before dinner, drinking cans of warm, cheap beer and blaring the television.

It had been converted into a family room, wood-panelled walls, shag rug, a garrison of dolls and toys. An abbreviated view of the crew-cut lawn.

Your brother would disappear; your father, edgy, would steal upstairs, mumbling something about pot-holders or place settings.

You and I would sit on the couch where you told me your mother had surprised you, many years ago, as a girl gave you head.

The minute I moved out, my parents painted over every remnant of my tenancy; my contempt.

I would sit gingerly on this couch—

remember your deaf grandfather screaming, During the war, women would have sex for cans of Spam!—

waiting to take my place at the table, my place in the silent dramas that simmered
there,

before me a plate of fiery red cabbage, tough meat, carefully drained of its blood.

I hated your poems—they made me jealous and irate,
because of their ardour and lies.

Expelled in a state of feverish conviction you would never
again experience,

encoded with your essence, and horribly so—

the eye of a crow, watchful, unblinking. Prepared to lay waste,
to plunder and scream, in envious outrage.

The eye of a fallen bird, filming over and broken.

Knowing distance and terror, and refusing to speak of it,
there are other exigencies.

Life coursing through you and passing over, like a calm,
shifting cloud.

A mathematical diagram of our time together would reveal
your efficiency with algebra, my failure at long division.

You walk up the stairs of our College Street apartment
with a handful of mail.

I ask you to relinquish a letter, its address girlishly rounded,
accented in rose and pink.

It is from one of your students. She confesses she wished she had protracted your
moment in the hallway; she wishes she had been bold enough to tell you

that yes, she would love to see you again,

that she hopes this finds you receptive to the idea.

I do not think of you teaching while making pointed eye contact
as John Donne demarcates his tears into continents,

entire worlds of longing.

I blame her entirely and ask you to respond accordingly.

You tell me you have chastised her, refused her kittenish overtures.

It will be seven years before it occurs to me you never again received a piece
of personal mail.

I thought you were unpopular.

Somehow hoping such moments could extrapolate—hallway
vectoring into highway,

unquantifiable variables, the strand of numbers spreading past the simple
point

that delineates the answer and its refutation,

my refutation, all of the answers you gave, that remain
inaccessible to me.

Initially, you left clues,
like a maniac on a killing spree,

who wants to be caught.

File folders labelled KRISTY or DONNA, unlocked boxes of porn.

My marauding put an end to this, and you closed up
like a spider.

Today I raked the last of the leaves and apples,
our dog,
my dog, Frank, running laps with his green ring, irritated.

You crossed my mind, as you do each time I am pressed to do something
odious and new.

You took care of everything—I do not remember anything but
a carpet of yellow and gold,

anything but this tableau disappearing, exposing wet earth,
lacerated, expectant.

I have since learned that expectation is synonymous with the worst
arrogance—

trees exfoliate and their leaves simply evanesce,

as it is distasteful to consider their decomposition; worse,
a commitment to the graft of attentiveness, care.

I wish that I had watched you at least, hefting up these
fallow piles, unsticking strays from the tines,

I wish that I had seen you, moving through the yard,
the backwards alchemy,

how you pushed us from season to season—

aching as soundlessly as the black boughs that surrendered
this intemperate mass.

You chose to be anonymous: this was your advantage and your affliction.

Like someone who is used to being declined; like someone who needs to escape
detection.

I would offer you anything; even the minutiae were refused: cheese sandwich, instant
coffee, a tensor bandage.

Larger gestures, obviated, headed off at the pass.

Refusing everything, as my caretaker and friend.

Refusing me also—

the mythology of need, devised by us both, whip-lashing me in the end.

I am standing on our porch, standing barefoot in the snow,
terrorized by what it is I think I know.

And, following me, you yell, You belong in an insane asylum.

Our neighbours mindful, my skin: hyacinth, iris.

Flowers the previous tenants left behind that force their way through
each spring,

oblivious to intention and origin,

showy and frail, unable to withstand the chance of climate.

Unseen, they streak forward and founder, against the weight of indiscernible winds.

From the start, I borrowed words to explain what I felt, that I was
wild with love

as I tore down your corridor, and beat at your door.

And we would latch together in the entrance, a bear and a bee.

Your sweetness: a song on an unlabelled mixed tape,
peaches, bananas, and everything good—

my first passion, falling in line with theft and larceny.
Flirtation preceded us, harmless, harmful.

I am walking down the pier at my boyfriend's cottage,
in a pink bikini, I am flipping my long red hair.

You are sitting on a chaise, everyone else is gone.

At the dock, I stumble, and right myself. Look back,
your eyes are unreadable, you indicate nothing.

I execute an exact dive among weeds and projecting rocks,
and surface.

This would be a story we shared, later.
A story about how desire is buried, like crates of silver,
like the bite of leeches,

below the surface of the proprietary water.

Cool air and sludge, the probability of garbage fish
sailing between your legs,

as sleek and unwelcome as your dark eyes, wanting,
appraising,

hiding from me.

I do not admit that you have ruined me,
that you changed my life,

as though swinging an axe.

That it is a combination of religion and drugs that walks me
from day to day,

discolouring my heart further,
as far as I have come.

It would surprise you, how seldom I think of you,
imagining you at this moment is like setting a radio dial to static,

a short, miscalculated wave.
Not hating you as much as what you have done—

You could be anyone.

Anyone who decides, for reasons unknown, to slide a blade inside his pocket,
whose cruelty is pointed yet arcane.

It has nothing and everything to do with you—the sight of your chipped black
bureau,
beside our bed,

gone one day, as if sliced from the floor.

The days and months, the time I spend—
like a woman troubling a disastrous decision,

closing my eyes, and opening them,
to find that it is still gone,

that our days will occasionally gorge into nightmares,

days begun with simple assumptions,

the maw of the alley, bright and clear,
the solidity of the bureau, each drawer heaving,

implicitly, with the gravity of your decision, to stay.

I tried to leave you right away,
afraid of your determination, certain of my need to be alone.

Your adamance and kindness, persuading me otherwise.

You would sit on my balcony like a ranch-hand,
gesturing to each acre I had left untilled.

Carrying a bag of hardware and a six-pack,
you made it seem possible,

unequivocally possible, to lasso the night's detritus:
little brilliants I could have at my disposal, a bracelet of charms.
And I leaned in, marginally closer,

and you reached for your Phillips head, and extracted a star.

I had seen you before.

You were performing in a park, in a pirate's shirt, and I was watching from the grass.

You were too pretty, your poems were experimental, urgent.

Like the inscriptions in old autograph books, *for u i pine*—

I have always distrusted beauty,
beauty without a rectifying deformity,

raw skin, a limp, a fang, insufferable accessories (black socks and beige shoes).

These lapses intimate love, the bald patches on a chair,

the more charming baldness of a lover who has just tremulously
started combing over.

Someone like you, I must have known, is not afraid of scrutiny.
Your flaws are unseen and indecipherable; the mirror,

its polished approbation, is enough.

In the last two years, and after that,
I began reading signs.
In the streets, the sky—

discarded origami, numbers, the sight of a cardinal,
picking at grass among the grackles,

a jet of language.

This morning I saw an open red suitcase, in the filthy park where
Frank and I walk,

lined with pink satin; inside, a child's white cotton nightgown.

In this same park, I have seen shrines of beer caps and pink tissue,
a tiny snowman with broken glass limbs;

A hawk, retreating to the tree-top; below,
a wreath of white feathers, enclosing a bloody heart.

I do not know who comes here at night: in the mornings, the shrub-roots
disclose syringes and distended rubbers.

I have come to draw my own conclusions. My life is,
at present, arrested.

Once I saw you on the street and watched you disappear.

The world is generous with its information; asking us to open
our eyes.

You had slipped back, I know now, to call her.

At the time, one of nature's prodigious skills was the ability
to obscure what I did not want to see.

Jealousy, my constant companion, grew flustered and decamped—
there was too much to absorb.

The first woman, I know only through letters.

An astrology-bug and photographer, who demonstrated faint concern
for me: *If you're sure that's what she wants*—

Or, Look at your horoscope today, it is just so amazing.

Or, When I was a little girl, I wanted to join the circus.

I seized her email address and wrote to her about your sign, Libra,
and mine.

I described a lion drowsing in the grass, by a metal scale.

You told me you had box seats for a game, asked if I minded you leaving.
Unusually solicitous, you offered to decline the invitation.

I watched the game with Frank, scanning the stands, missing you.

There had been courtesy beverages and sandwiches, you said, returning home
with a program and a plush Carlton.

You remarked on the fight in the last seconds of play.

Later, you would tell me you had gone there, and left immediately
with your clutch of evidence.

Gone to your girlfriend's and slept with her for the first time.

The fight had erupted out of tension and failure.

Everyone stood up and I did not see you: this seemed immaterial,
as I saw what you saw,

heard the slap of dropped gloves, jerseys wrenched off.

The first punch thrown never makes contact: its arc simply shaping what
the game has come to, that it will end.

You used to stand in front of windows, staring.

It drove my family crazy—you at your station, high above
Sherbrooke Street, and there were raised whispers,

What the hell is he doing?

I don't know, I told them. Later, you would tell me you were afraid of heights,
therefore mesmerized.

There is some truth to this, like all lies.

I knew otherwise. Lonely, exhausted with your own demeanor, you would
watch the cars pressing through snow, the fleet crushes of passers by,
and feel like their Doppler effect,

what is vivid yet left behind—

you would graze against that window and dare yourself to fall
like a comet and be noticed, and named.

We moved off of College, just north of the noise.
You found this place to appease me, and it never appeased me,

the noise of the street replaced by grotesque domestic concerns—

a python-sized worm in the shower drain,
the shower that abutted the laundry room where six inches of black
sludge pooled,

the windowsill in the basement kitchen an entomologist's workshop,
where platter-sized spiders captured coaster-sized beetles,

the mushroom blooming between the cracks in blackened parquet tiles,
more viscous and garish each time.

It grew beside the cupboard that was forever dis-hinging itself,
and we found ourselves there, one day, and you said,

I will never leave you,

and the mushroom's black cap swayed,

as you held me and I believed you,

it asserted itself, and sounded like a bell.

I wanted to ask you—

what it felt like to leave. When you visited, a visitor suddenly,
and ripped off strip after strip of packing tape.

Rolls of tape tumbling around, picked clean, and bone-white.

When the moving men came they were slow and poky, until my grief
became apparent.

Then they moved like paramedics, handling each box like a limp body in a
burning house.

You showed less alacrity, asking me if I had a "star screwdriver" to remove the bannister.

Torn between pain and contempt, I handed it to you, and watched you leave,
with all of the tools you could not identify,

drills and drivers, chuck keys and planes—

these were mine, if seldom accessed.

The hacksaw that you used to trash dead branches.

As you retreated, I stood in the room and held out
my arms, among the standards of light.

There was an entire week.

Between the night you told me you wanted to leave and your departure.

Trapped and vicious, you extended faint hope. If I could only—

I felt exhilarated, cleaned the walls and baked banana bread.

One night, a storm caught hold and I sunk to the floor. You were in your room, refusing
to talk: I knew nothing, other than your intentions.

I called my friend and castigated him for not paying closer attention. Met him
on the corner, in the blizzard,

endured his small talk, graceless pats on the head and one piece of good advice:

There is always someone else, he said. Let's call her Brenda. And when things
are going badly, we think: It would be better with Brenda.

And we spend our entire lives thinking of Brenda, who is of course,
not better than Brenda.

He put me to bed in a cupboard; as a courtesy, left incense burning in the reeking
cat-litter box, five sticks of saffron and peach underlining the ammonia.

I tried to break into your voice mail. Your code was LOVE; you'd changed it.

Got up as the sun rose, and walked home, and watched trucks unloading loaves of bread,
awnings raising, the street curving home.

This is my home, I thought, gathering Frank and refusing to tell you where I had been.

Frank sighed and plumped himself beside me.

The next day I would throw you out, laying claim to this place,
the site of my unhappiness,

the site of what you determined to be my unhappiness,
yours, all along.

Your anaphylaxis made me vigilant—
I was anxious about restaurants, labels, hidden toxins,

a friend's desire to cook with peanut oil.

The mere taste of it, lingering in my mouth like cyanide—

I carried an Anakit and you did not,

locked and loaded with epinephrine and chalky
orange pills.

I remember the night you came over, claiming you were
all right, and when I turned the lights on your head was pumpkin sized.

The constant threat of emergency that you took in stride.

Your mother made a peanut casserole and we spent hours in the hospital,

eventually, I left with your brother and watched *Touched by an Angel*
with your parents and aunt,

trying to get along with them,

I asked if Della Reese was God; feigned alarm when Nell Carter
torqued herself into a small car.

When we retrieved you, you snapped at me in the car.

And this was one of the many end runs—

You, juiced up with the antidote I gave you, flipping through wrestler magazines
and scarfing the double cheeseburger I brought to your bedside,

while I watched this show in the morgue; that is,
the basement,

of your parents' bombed-out shelter.

Our lives became as insular as a can of vacuum-packed peanuts,
which, when opened, hisses incredulously.

I made a new friend, eventually. Six feet tall and traffic-stopping,
she showed up at our place in a two-inch miniskirt and stiletto boots.

Later, you said how nice it was, to watch us walking down the street,
that I had someone to talk to.

She would visit me again, breach the apartment where we never
admitted anyone,

because we were ashamed, because our isolation was a contract,
never spoken of, iron-clad.

In a white leather dress and bare feet, she would discover our stereo,
turn its dial past its radius,

and dance like Shiva:

You should learn how to say no!

We took pictures of each other. She is a bolt of lightning. I sink into the pillows,
wary, and gaunt.

This was like sage, this was like sorcery.

This was like undoing each term and caveat—
It was nice to watch her—

You should learn.

How to stop speaking, how lies emerge, dependent on unspeakable clauses,
how fragments form, in syntactical infractions,

in a refusal to deny what is half-said—

conjunctive adverbs, detaching like missiles in orbit,
through mischance, igniting,

burning everything in their wake.

You visited the press where I worked; we were proposing an anthology
of writers who were shuffled back in the deck like twos or aces.

The publisher had just had a baby.
And you held this baby in hands that seemed suddenly expansive;
your face a study in piety,

these catechetical fingers,

latching onto you.

The publisher the age I am now; her baby would be nine years old.

Marked by scars that do not include the touch of your hands,

cradling him—

the baby in the manger, and the Orient's ambassadors,
bearing gifts that, like unbroken horses,

rear up, discharging their freight,
and without design, tear away.

You never wanted to get married and this suited me,
until I felt slighted by your disinclination.

Years before, you had my name tattooed to your chest,
in the font of one of my books' titles,

in a heart prised from an art book I had given you.

A metaphysical demonstration that we *more than married* were.

I was unmoved by the tattoo, certain of its impermanence.

What if you inscribe an insult below it, I asked? (thinking of John Lydon in
a Pink Floyd T-shirt, above it scrawled I HATE),
or laser it, or black it out?

Strike a line through it—

The Scotchgarded cushions of your mother's couch, the letters you deleted,
the pain you withheld,

underneath it all, something screaming to be heard,

honesty, dirty and itinerant—
the man who slept in our hallway, wrapped in my quilt. Tired of him
endangering us, with his episodes and little bonfires,

you chased him into the streets screaming, *never come back*,
and he did not.

I saw him once, lurking in the alley, the blanket tossed across his shoulder.

Toreador—he slipped into the advancing night, and now I am fanciful,
I am cold enough to imagine roses,

sodden beneath the dark appraisal of his retreat.

There were three of us, and we discovered a shopping cart left derelict
at the crossroad,

on the way to the party, where we will appear together, for the first time.

From a distance, we can see writers in the window, dancing, badly, to what will
turn out to be Human League.

Later, we will try to play Drunk Operation with a man in diamante pants;
you will enter the bathroom with me and piss, luridly, for the first and last time,
your leg pretzeled.

My friend and I took turns riding in the cart and at your turn, we manoeuvred you
into heavy traffic, shoved, then turned to each other and said,
Let go.

You careened through cars and streetcar tracks until the cart
heaved over, disgorging you,

injured and furious.

It was an accident, I would argue. It has been nine years, and still, I know,

like dropping a hamster in a makeshift parachute from a balcony,

it was, and it was not.

I have, at times, held my head in my hands,
and told myself it will be all right.

A lie that I miss.

I have wrapped the sleeves of a shirt around my shoulders;
bumped against a wall, sinking into its solidity.

I know better,

Frank knows better, when he purls himself against my stomach
and moos,

knitting his infancy together,

stumbling into dreams.

You had travelled extensively, and I resented this,
as every trip seemed to occasion a poem

about kissing at the Wailing Wall,
or wishing you had kissed at the Wailing Wall.

This made me feel like a croupier on the Pacific Princess who is not permitted
to make day trips,

just deal cards with a practised, tenebrous hand.

As if you were the early Dylan Thomas and I were the late Dylan Thomas,

your excursions a pink nimbus, washed in orange, and orange and red;
my own, the plotted course between sleep and wakefulness.

You went to Christ's sepulchre, and felt something of His covenant.

On my road trips, I stop at the roadhouses, and the old men and I thank God!
when the first beer arrives, filling space,

and breathing ice until the bottle sweats prayers.

A cube of sugar in the hands of a raccoon,
who cleans it until it dissolves.

This is not love—a friend once told me, after a while, it's not the petting,
but the grooming we come to value.

The absurd amount of money I spent on clothes and jewellery for you,
a black suit, a rainbow of shirts, a solitary diamond.

The man I loved before you had a brother who used to cut himself
open, then sew over what he had buried there.

I think of this solitaire jewel, cut under my name, cut under the erasure,
how mythologies occur, Atlantis,

parallel worlds.

The salesman was named Foster Hewitt, not *the* Foster Hewitt.

I asked him to wrap the diamond with his card,
which I thought would please you.

I am standing at Birks, fully aware that whatever authenticity is absent will manifest
itself in the shine and the story,

the penalty Gretzky never received for high-sticking Gilmour, in a game we watched
before we met,

a game we lamented, separately, your anguish, of course, more acute.

The Leafs have not won a Stanley Cup since the year you were born.

The diamond was a covenant, and I think of it now,
still shining,

divorced of its meaning, the crude remnants of a mass of coal, refined and polished,

shining its coarse intentions—maybe next year,

we would deserve the win.

How do you explain your belongings to her?

Ornate boxes upon boxes, privacy, extended nervously to you.

Long after you left, I loaded you with presents, including my own desk,
its surface marked with half-circles, other contusions.

I thought of you as my executor, the only physician accountable for my vital statistics,
the force of my sentiments,

no longer bearable.

I imagine her saying that the desk doesn't work with the new place,
see you labouring to haul it all to the street.

Just as easily as I see you burying me in the shallows of her backyard, making room
for daffodils and peonies—

sentiment is not transferable.

It is as though I asked you to safeguard a bag of stones; and, in doing so,
asked you to care about each one,

its resemblance to Mercury, to the curve of your cheek, to the fungus that broke
through our floor,

insistent and ugly: how it consecrated what you said, and how you lied.

A friend complained to me tonight the second he closes his eyes,
his wife wants to talk about plans,

where they will travel,

the condition of the portobello mushrooms, the clump of the cat
litter.

I thought of you, listening to me rail about the shredded wallpaper,
the neighbour's clogs, a litany of what I then perceived as squalor.

How you absorbed this, as you sank into the cushions, how I return to you,
on faint feet,

and see how like a jonquil you are; that I adore you.

I had not spoken to Janet for years, she was married,
trying to have children—I would hear from him.

Calls inviting us to go skating, a Halloween or New Year's party,
things we never did.

Eventually, he sent me photographs of the view from their trailer, on Lake Lingerlong,
outside of Parry Sound.

I wouldn't have bothered asking you to go.

When Janet and I met she was drawn and changed.

Things are fine, she told me. We went to see the Friendly Giant exhibit at CBC,
saw Rusty and Jerome,

un-handed, inert,

and had a drink one block away from where I am now. I thought,
Who would want to live here?

Janet would call me, a month later, and tell me her marriage was over. Since that
time, I have watched her box of Kleenex migrate, from the dashboard
to the backseat,

never to the trunk.

You and I went to a New Year's party once and you drank straight vodka
you said was water and ogled a girl in salmon pink.

When you stared at the girl, I could hardly blame you. Time was passing—
as we walked and fought home,

the snow fell in plain sheets,
telling me, telling us what would break us,

what would make us stronger.

Janet's husband left in an eddy of lies,

We were never happy; I wanted a child: she could not give me one—
there is no one else.

I saw no one else,

when I visited the trailer beside hers, not hers anymore.

His new girlfriend was slinking to the wharf like a rodent:
I could not apprehend what he had taken from her, in his absence.

The last time they were together, he held a pillow over her face as the moon waxed,
and said, It's too bad you look so good.

We picked through the stones to her car and burned rubber,
this one moment, stolen—

from his possessions, the leeches and tensile weeds of the lake,
the sheen of the trailer's aluminum sides, Janet's empty eyes.

As if he was taking liminal measure, of what belonged to him.

You were fascinated by this break-up, its circumstances,
the practicalities,

you cornered Janet on my birthday with a sympathy that
offended her,

pressing for details.

I was puffy and indeterminate, the kind of state that can go either way.
Where love or hate can drag you, behind its certain velocity.

As a scientist, you chose empirical proofs of wormholes, detours,
exits.

As a scientist, I rested on method—cake, admiration, your apparent
discomfort with betrayal,

or equivocal love,

where lies and truth excuse each other, in service of a higher equation.

One which, in higher realms, is reductive and unvarying.

The taste of your sweat, say; the pitch
of your snoring.

Your body could sustain such irregularities,
your body was created this way,

all that I have ever known beauty to be.

It is precisely a year since we have spoken.
Your number is listed,

listed under her name.

I could call or write you anytime,
in your own parole: diminutive personal pronouns,

extrapolating into a sentimentality about dead singers,
missed opportunities,

the dire experience of banging on a door when the corpse inside
is unable to answer (penance—the inscription of a painful, ambiguous tattoo).

I am thinking now,

in this cold place, as Frank leaps on and off me, suspicious and neglected,
of your lower case personal pronouns.

The small "I" you favoured, fenced in with ampersands,
I am wondering why,

A calculated hesitation about topic and subject,
a child's idea of what looks pretty on the page.

I told you, when I first saw your cover design, that it

suggested borrowed nostalgia; worse, it barely resembled you.

The militia of grass spears in the jungle of your desiring, effectively undone by the solipsism
that stimulates confession,

I wish I had said, why don't you call this LOVE ME.

Instead I grabbed your James Dean cigarette case, and defaced it,
overscoring his name with that of a criminal's,

asking you sincerely if you were serious—

these people mean nothing to you.

Culpable too. You mean nothing to me, and it is late and I am tired,
and you are somewhere like a lily,

not toiling or spinning,

and I am alone, remembering you, as if constructing a poor collage,
of stars and immortals,

of men who step away and accelerate, their precision consecrated in the
mash of metal and blood.

You told me stories about growing up I could never repeat,
for the transgression,

because I have forgotten,

because these are your own stories to tell.

I had always hoped they would illuminate your silence, a memory of duct tape,
and barbed wire.

Instead, I heard about trophies accumulating like head lice,
countless victories,

playing left wing with a broken hand and still slotting
the five-hole,

before your hand, released from the glove, cabbaged into fracture.

The trophies filled your room, spilling into the basement,
a testimony to ambition and failure,

what you came to care about was never acknowledged,

your books slid into recessed shelves, their spines backwards,
unbroken.

Your parents measured success like the handfuls of salt your mother would
blizzard into her mock-Irish stew,

like the idiotic golden hands of the squash or lacrosse player,
whose posture suited the erect ears of the bunnies and babies

lined posthumously there.

Your most ambitious book did not merit this display, I never saw it in their home,
yet you dedicated it to her,

for her strength and support—

When I graduated your father called me and asked me to inspire you
to "get off the punt."

I should not have been so weak. He was fascinated by very little,
soccer and shipwrecks.

Such correlations draw lines in the orange shag
dividing your small aspirations from his,

neither possible, one better—it is the effort in spite, in spite of what is worthy,
and tawdry, and meant.

You're in suspension—

I was writing a novel before, as one of the Manson Family once said,
it all came down.

I was consumed by my material, a boy I once loved, long dead,
who returned to me in veins of light,

who haunted me.

Someone made me a bag, a superstitious scrap of velvet,
noosed with a silver dog.

The dreams persisted—

In hindsight, I knew, I was losing you.

But I cannot return to anything but this story, that begins and ends
in your absence.

I alluded to it in a story that was rejected for its opaque structure.

In the section about you, you are named Shane. It is dishonest and refers
to you, and the lies we told, over a year ago, together:

> This morning as I walk my dog—a sullen man is packing his car trunk,
> suitcases, twined boxes, paper bags. I hear a woman scream a boy's name.
> A boy darts into the street toward the man, cars brake. His mother follows,
> holding a plate of fried eggs, their edges frilled and blackened. You know
> he always follows you! she cries. Why? she adds. She is crying. The man is
> oblivious, yells something about his keys. The boy's eyes follow.
> This man's name is not Shane.
>
> In this story he is the father, and you are the mother, and you are the boy.

I have spent this long looking for your opposite,
revelling in cruel men who not only look for fights but mean it—

you would be occasionally protective, if the man in question was out of earshot,
or lamentably tiny.

You came home one day, long into our separation (named only in hindsight,
by me)

and told me a story:

This guy was yelling at me from his car for not moving fast enough
and I told him to step outside, You fat bastard, let's go. And he *backed down*.

How old was he, I asked.

He was in his seventies as it turned out, and I asked you if being called a fat
bastard would not make you haul ass, and shrivel against the lime
green of your Plymouth.

Your fists still clenched as you recited the story, his anger and retreat,
any antagonist, the argot the same, weaker, stronger—

my wish that you had been stronger; how you undid this wish,
by showing me that you had failed,

that you would fail again,

unable to decipher parity,

for its allegations, for what it wants.

My parents moved to a tropical island, oddly, incredibly.

Broke the news to us in Kensington Market—I could barely believe the
audacity.

We would visit them and you would carry me through the sea like Johnny Weismuller,
on the plane to Miami, separated, I looked at you, an aisle away,

and envied myself, if that is possible.

Honey-coloured, and strange. My reflection in your mirrored glasses,
the things we saw at the Seaquarium,

stingrays and gelatinous spikes, bivalves outfitted like centurions,

ugly enough that I asked you to carry me through them,
where they spawn and where they lurk.

You were the one who could get things fixed,
virulent computers, low-fi stereos,

toasters ejecting flaming slices of rye.

You carried an Army Surplus bag filled, I assumed, with
micro-drivers and welding torches.

You actually saluted when you left,
as if tipping a cap, as if welding the Arc of the Covenant.

This sort of thing is irresistible when an eyelash curler seems
like a prop from *Dead Ringers,*
when an eavestrough is not only full, but is an *eavestrough,*

when you absolutely need to write a poem about snails,
and your keyboard is jammed on asterisks and percentages.

The secret to women's helplessness is ingenuity. I retrieved my
screwdrivers by accusing an ape of fixing my doors,

while making a baked Alaska and a tourniquet.

My culpability matched by your overweening helpfulness.

Later, much later, we would both damn ourselves for refusing
to say no,

like watching a grilled cheese sandwich curl at the edges and implode.

This is not a skill,

it is the dangerous brinkmanship that comes to define love—
the slop of ketchup on the side,

pooling.

Like broken vessels, an astronomy of refusal,
choke on it.

I have not written since the beginning, the mania that first defined
my solitude,

shovelling first the stairs then half the street; burning though crossword puzzles,
suddenly possessed of a vocabulary of single-vowel words

beginning with x and ending with Q;

deciding to finish a novel, a mystery about a French detective
and his sidekick, a surprisingly vulgar half-formed twin growing out of his abdomen.

I would wake up at five, running Frank into the advancing light,
making plans, model dinosaurs,

a doll house in a matchbox, white-flocked, plaster genitals
as described in *Era Amante de Michael Jackson,*

clay pigeons, a wooden Howitzer.
I remember your conditions, spread out before me,
uneasily, reasons you may stay—

how I hauled the upright vacuum into the bedroom immediately,
and managed to make that thing climb walls.

As though you would run a white-gloved finger across the baseboard,
affected by an admiration that, if overblown,

would turn into love.

I have one of your books beside me, the Jesus one.
Your eyes are at half-mast, whiting against a scrim of clouds.

As though Christ was killed by a peanut allergy.

In extremis, He spread His arms against the dusty husks
of His enemy,

forgiving them,

of all the lethal, sparking things that are concealed within
the blandness of cookie dough or the dumb trunk of an elephant,

like bad intentions,
like rumours, treachery, and passion.

You hid your fanatical devotion to hockey for years.

If I came across you watching TV you would switch channels;

when you subscribed to an atrocious newspaper, I assumed
you were secretly obsessed with automotive information.

And when I ferreted out your hard-core dedication to the Leafs,
I played along. Watched every game with you,

grasping, painfully, through demonstrations involving a bottle cap
and record sleeve,

the meaning of icing, off-sides, high-sticking, instigator-penalties, good checks,
bad checks, two-pad rollovers.

The only thing one ever has to understand about the Leafs is that
whenever they lose, they actually win,

because they outplayed the other team, because of bad calls,
and worse luck.

When Italy lost the World Cup to Brazil, the Italian fans gathered along
St. Clair yelled adamantly, We are still Number One!

No, I thought. Idly watching Portuguese fans from my window,
leading livestock down College and blazing with victory.

No, that would make you Number Two.

My brother, like your brother, had a marriage end in a tempest of
lies—

recorded visits to psychics, cryptic calls, hotel charges,
the usual manoeuvres.

And he was right there, before you moved and after,
as you pulled off the bannister to heave your things,

the things I packed so carefully, deranged with the kind of hatred
that can only lacerate inward.
He sat with me and said, This is the worst of it.

I did not eat for a week. He slept in my basement, cooked me things
I would push aside; finally made a plate of crackers and salami,

each slice decorated with mustard faces, smiling.

I lay on my bed staring at the plate as if it was spring-loaded,
seized it and ate every crumb.

Somehow this nourished me more than anything anyone could do or say;
nourishes me still,

that chipped plate crowded,

like the Indian women I saw in the park this morning dancing in a circle
to a sitar, turning and stamping,

crowded with ritual and the joy that I only find
by accident, and that was among the best of what I remember.

I could only listen to two records, every other song seemed to be
screaming at me, pointedly: *How does it feel? To be on your own?*

Velvet Underground Three, and *Sticky Fingers*,
something about their sedative complaints,

and congruent misery.

"Wild Horses" taking precedence: how I would buy you what
you wanted, as if that might stay your displeasure.

You had a locked room at the end of the hall, which became filled
with this effluence,

posters, KISS magnets, a guitar, tickets to games and wrestling matches—
in effect, a teenage boy's sanctuary,

unconsciously designed as a corollary to your actual room,
and its violable signals of achievement and straight aspiration.

I did not know that I was telling you, not to regress, but to live
for your own pleasure,

at my expense, to my detriment.

I had forgotten what is was like, to be that young. To hole up, unable to recognize
that the bequest of pure privacy breeds contempt,

the desire to kick out the doors of the stall, rear up, bolt,

because you have not been groomed for show,

but to tear like a streak, unfettered and wild,
through the dark woods,

breaking new earth and branches, breaking out.

Television, movies, books: this was more of the same. I was suspicious
of everything static, everything inherently volatile.

For a long time, I lived like Algernon, liberated of an intelligence that felt
more inherited than true,

sweeping dirt into piles, scraping it back.

I lost a lot of friends.

It is unpleasant to see people change. It feels contagious,
it feels as if it is their own fault.

The dirt continued to accumulate, my fault.

I could have been more vigilant, I should have known
better,

what arises in neglect.

Long before, I had warily approached the drain of our filthy shower
and reached in and pulled.

Rearing up from the handfuls of soap-grimed hair, an undulating worm—

Lying is motile, it migrates back and forth, leaving marks.

Your lies, examined later, are like the yellow streaks and cavities
that discolour photographs and books.

This comparison is inexact, as wear and tear are honest
representations, signals that time is inimical to purity,

that love injures itself in order to be exact.

You lied differently; that is, with barely a trace.

I had to examine our life together as though applying Luminol,
for the invisible vestiges of blood.

The green jet exposing carnage, in each instance.

I thought of friends I had, who lived in lofts on Liberty Street,
who painted and wrote songs,

strung up Tiki lights and styled hair,

held court in wedding gowns, hauling down sleep onto button-tufted
futons,

as the trucks lined up each week, unloading pigs,
as the men in white gowns herded them inside.

Only one of these friends ever heard them screaming;
to this day, she is consumed by the sound,

one of the rare people who, when she feels her heart pounding,
is faint with love, with an apprehension of the organ's function,

how it extends and contracts, in each swinish modulation.

Genuine pain will make you contemptuous of the idea of s/m,
with its safe-words; its implicit devotion

to the straight rigours of knowledge.

A week in, I was asking you to arrest an agony I thought you owned.

I once stepped on a woman on a bus. My stiletto pierced her shoe,
and it hurt.

I'm sorry, I'm sorry I said.

She felt better when I retracted my heel, and that is our unvarnished
love story—
if there is a scar, she has forgotten; if there is a scar, I am sorry.

You came to meet me at my hairdresser,
among the girls in platform boots and slip-dresses,

sewing extensions in the thunder of "The Immigrant's Song,"

and told one of them, Cut it off.

I knew that it would suit you but felt a pang I still feel,

as your cultivated curls fell like sleet,

I thought of *Hammer of the Gods*, in the manner of Jimmy Page
who you no longer resembled.

Vaguely explained by him as an instrument and aspect,
guitar strings, a veil of hair

whipping through power chords like a spell.

You will talk to me less, eventually clam up,
cultivating a language I cannot speak.

I feel. Married. Buried.

You were a Kurt Cobain fan; we took three buses to see
the Nick Broomfield movie, never talked about it.

If we were to speak now, I would talk to you about your eyes,
those dark peonies,

tar pits, sunken repositories—entire continents.

I kept the movie poster and his eyes are so sad,
I have turned it to face the wall.

I wonder how this could have escaped me—

I am in the country, sledding from a hill into the foundation of a building.

The landing sends tremors through my spine: under the film of snow,
the expanse of dirt, there is nothing.

Light, streaking through you, falling away.

The bureau was one of the rare remnants of a past relationship

(You came to me, as men do, empty-handed.)

Your ex-girlfriend had acquired it for you at a junk store, and painted
it in ten layers of glossy black, polished the silver pull-handles
into moonlight.

An object I found hateful, for its irregular surfaces, sagging interior,
the way that its drawers captured sock ends and collars, like rat snakes.

When you left, I would lie on the bed, and close my eyes. Open them,
desperate to see the bureau, cry over its loss, as much as anything.

When I moved, its absence moved with me.

I think of your girlfriend, betrayed by both of us, painting it with tar
and deadly nightshade,

leveraging the drawers, so that they would remain ajar
and capture everything you thought, that I thought, was secreted away.

I never kissed anyone else, nothing happened.
That is, in its own way, a lie.

My unfaithful heart inflated between us, pushing us to either end
of the bed.

One particular man—

I saw him last night. He is married, happy.

I told him I felt like Lucifer these days, *Paradise Lost*,
third book.

He has not read it. He's miserable, he said. But he can still fly around.

I tried to explain his particular affliction, familiar to anyone whose
personality is like a crate of insects and dirt.

I demonstrated the point instead, by sitting in his lap, and telling him
he smelled like gardenias and rosewater.

Just flew into his arms, and he held me, awkwardly,
as the air around us grew heavy with deception, the weight of our past.

This man had seen you recently, thought you looked well, brimming
over with poems and plans,

and all I felt about you was that I wished I could be you, that I could lie.

I wish I could lie about you, is what I mean.

To walk to the church, where Frank and I go each day, and look at the cross
and swear I forgive you.

All the pigeons berthed there would soar past us, singing,
and I could feel as clean as the concrete wading pool,

I would be the flower mandala, painted in its centre.

God shies away from my refusal; I am certain He would also despise that lie.

You were not an atheist exactly. You thought God was an energy,
a criss-crossing spirit of goodness,

never to be defined.

I called you a hippie, and we argued, long into the night.

We would sit on the balcony and fight, and these fights were fair,
and unclaimed.

To the right of this balcony was a Baptist church. I used to go to their
bazaars, and buy distressed rayon skirts and garish blouses.

One night, a parishioner burned it to the ground.

Our hamster had just died, Honey. We loved her excessively,
to the bemusement of most,

who had never seen her, angrily arranging walnuts or linen handkerchief,
learning to climb the stairs between her pink house and balcony,
the way she curled into my hand, your hand, like a little pulse.

It was time to move, I decided. Our neighbours below us were also packing,
between fights.

He was a meat packer and she was a pious Spanish girl and they fought,
and they screamed until she had to sit on the stairs,

and they made up sometimes in a flurry of amorous assaults,

and he told her, We come from the apes, and she told him,

We come from God.

Before I left, she had just moved out. He came upstairs and told me he
used to work in the Maritimes on a fishing boat, dressed like Elton John.

He gave me a package of cold cuts, and read my poems.
He was pretty drunk. He said, How do you. Think like that.

Before the church was gutted there were sunny days. He and I drank
beer and talked intermittently, about what we could never understand.

Evolution and miracles,

trawling for fish in ten-inch platforms; insisting that God is not
a spirit or creator,

but a traffic director, toughing out inclement weather with three signs,
signs we ignore or obey—

the rain and snow obscure His face and we obscure Him also;
we have places to go,

it costs us, to stop; more, to yield.

I wonder if we had stayed, would you have stayed.

You found the last apartment, charmed the almost-slumlord, and charmed me also.

The day we moved in, I had to be restrained from telling the movers to go back.

The tenants had left holes in the ground, securing their rose bushes; a home-made bong; Mason jars; stacks of magazines; a steaming, filled diaper.

The walls were pocked with holes, disfigured with their attempts at home decorating:

piss-yellow walls, rubbed over with a paper bag; the stairs kamikaze'd with silver; the parquet tiles detaching like puzzle pieces.

My friends were quiet, getting us in. It's not really you, one of them said, noting the high-gloss brown cabinets of the kitchen,

the pathetic bar that bisected the basement, virtually begging for stools and an amusing sign:

I don't have a drinking problem. I drink and fall down. No problem!

Neither of us drank, sitting together was out of the question.

Your grandfather had a mouldering bar in his basement, with neon Löwenbräu signs, jars of swizzle sticks, and a surplus of rum in various proofs.

When he died, you took the bar signs, and hid them in your room: I had long since filled the bar with bowls and plates,

some idea of a trousseau; some idea of moving along, eventfully.

We were foolish and we squandered something convulsively beautiful, for the shame.

My new friends showed off the basements of their houses, laughing at the monstrosity, effectively, our place.

That we began to care was the first and most awful error.

When you left, I had a party that began at the bar, and never faltered.

We never knew how to flaunt our difference, and these differences would divide themselves, into your lies, spun from the recesses of your room,

into mine—aggrieved pride manifesting itself as seclusion, when it was shame,
when there was no reason, when we both should have known better.

Something like Zero Mostel yelling out his window at a flashy car, while failed but striving,
Flaunt it baby.

Something like that.

I called my mother and read her the poem about the pickles.
Why are they walking on pickle-legs? she asked.

It's a *metaphor*, I said. Realizing it was not, that your mother's taste
was infectious,

her desire to enclose things that cannot escape; little creatures
that are mobile only in narrative.

My mother has never made brine. If you give her something cute,
she will move it to the basement,

where my father dispatches such things.

She may hate the analogy, but if confronted with pickles,
they would roll from the jar and burgeon into cucumbers,

hale and greening—she has known for some time, how to let go.

My intimates these last two years have been cab drivers; somehow,
our conversation always steers to this—My husband left me,

he was having two affairs.

These men are always taken aback by the numbers; one,
empathic in the extreme, cried and said, I feel like it's happening to me!

Others have scrawled their numbers on the receipt, or cursed
the weakness of men.

They often have large families; I often think of them this way.

You were never my husband, but you insisted this was what you wanted.

It was not what I wanted, but the less interest you showed, the more I campaigned.

You told me, as if forced to reveal your hand, that you had been saving
money in a shoebox for over a year,

loose change and folding money, all towards a diamond ring.

I would discover this box never existed: this was one of your better lies,
tangible, and fugitive.

I had imagined this box so many times, its loose freight.

The darkness of its interior—

I have sat in a taxi, long after the meter has stopped,
talking to a driver named Remy,

his face in the darkness, averted, lustrous with scars,
talking quietly,

each scar a jewel, shining, telling me what is valuable,
that the cost is inestimable, and cradled in pain.

Nothing happened—

I dreamed he met me at Customs, and held me;
woke up holding myself.

We drove to Parry Sound, and shared a seatbelt coming back,
listening to "Candy's Room,"

sighing, the gulls on the beach that strafed our sandwiches,
how his eyes looked like goldfish,

the sound of his voice.

As quiet as the sand that shifted as we moved together and away,
the lake turfing up yellow bile,

the moon pausing like an usher, before flashing forward,
and separating us.

After the Leafs' sixth or so playoffs choke, you turned to
the WWF, and managed to get me involved, to some extent,

in the story lines, a game I had followed in Montreal,
through Andre the Giant and Gilles "The Fish" Poisson.

My grandmother used to go to matches when Coconut Willie
was a contender, other shockingly named stars,

most of them disaffected, performing in a larger theatre, the world.

I bought us tickets to WrestleMania for Valentine's Day, and bought a Stone Cold
Steve Austin foam finger, and we took our places among the eleven-year-old boys
and their indulgent parents.

There was a young couple behind us—the girl kept asking who the bad
guys were, and then made hissing sounds, a tiny sibilant sssssssss.

In the washroom, I jockeyed in line among girls in masks and body paint,
returned to the crushing boredom of table-smashes and oily hammerlocks,

pathetically hoisting the finger.

You fought with me about something, I forget what.

I cannot forget my acute embarrassment, how I cried there—

I am too reserved to wear chandelier earrings, but you yelled at me
in front of the sleepy kids and the snake girl, in front of her indulgent boyfriend,

the man sailing Eskimo Pies from row to row.

Manners rarely make sense: the motion of a soup spoon, elbows on the table.

Retaining logic, the premise secluded:

Never yell at anyone in a wig, or large hat, or foam finger—
the costume makes its own assumptions about tolerance.

We were looking for a house, with money we had pulled out of thin air.

I hated every one you showed me, finally agreed to go see the one on Shaw
half-sunk into the ground, all of the interior furnishing battened down;

the house with aluminum siding *inside*; the converted garage with dry-walled partitions
and alley views,

the one house you swore I would love—you brought home a Polaroid, and I was
hopeful, fleetingly, for its abstract tininess and window boxes, teeming with pansies
and geraniums.

There was no room for you there, you insisted you would work in the basement
under the pipe leaks, among the metropolis of wires, ducts and furnace-extremities.

The vendor was clearly nervous; among her few belongings was a photograph of her fiancé,
obviously clipped from a magazine.

Who lives next door, I asked, as she urged us to wander the twenty feet of backyard
tiles.

Oh, a very nice family. The father is in an eclectic klezmer band. The walls were puckered,
from enraged poundings, I could hear one of many children bash against them,

see their impressions, like pummelled clay.

I hate it, I told you, and your friend, the wan realtor, who tended to slide her eyes towards you,
sympathetically,

as the neighbours struck up a lively *freylach* that lifted the roof.

You were already seeing someone else—but still intent on seeing this through.

A room for me and a hovel for you, where you could discharge the last of your
obligations among the spiders and millipedes,

writing morose letters, that blamed me, in the style of the *tanzen*
that would enter our home,

in my case, like a riotous *simcha*; in yours, the aching strains of a violin.

A close friend is going through something with her husband. Although she
was kind to me, I cannot bring myself to help,

because it is too hard to watch, because this has changed me.

I side more easily with aggressors,

I am tired of watching women who, in their terror of being left,
are changed also.

Large women, as insistent as thunder, made small,
their allure recast as repulsion,

all of them looking for dust in corners, freezing sauces,
probing themselves with sharp instruments.

Like a lamb outfitted in the skin of its dead offspring, I chase
the one who has the power to starve me, or leave me behind.

With the rest of the women—we would wash the floors of Hell itself,
if we could find the answer there,

in the waxy surface—

what we lost and why we ever thought it was ours.

You're not a happy person, you said. I want to be happy.

I lacked the presence of mind to tell you that you are approximately as joyous
as death row,

that you were not looking for that, and never had.

I did understand that certain implosions are gratifying, that deception itself
is pleasing, because it alters you, entirely.

Then things resume, as they were.

We shared an approximate happiness, in the kind of order best compared
to the compass of a lint brush,

in deepest secrecy.

I almost like to think of you finding some chaotic pleasure in undoing
everything you are,

in the occasional moments I remember as tedious to you.

Six feet of new snow that I ran into, sinking. How Frank navigated the backyard,
making boughs of cherries appear, a row of tulips,

the night I slipped off a fence and held my face to yours, laughing.

Before you composed yourself, I saw that I disgusted you, and was ashamed.

It was that night you told me you were unhappy; that I was.

Your face stormy with misery, my own, gathering your hard rain,
until I resembled you, until the slow, pallid arrival of a light
you could not camouflage, or contain.

I dreamed the other night that you told me, I'm just going to clean
my room, and do drugs with your ex.

Fine, I said, that is fine.

I was preoccupied with a half-dressed and earnest man.
When I came to see you, you were gone. The room emptied, other than a few
photographs, dust, a closet filled with brown shirts.

You did come to clean out your room, then. Swiped at the dusty shelves, and cleared
everything but a Styrofoam cup and a garbage bag,

its lip numinous with dust; among this, a tiny leather jacket—
the first gift I ever gave you.

In the dream you are also two inches tall, working the jacket's
little zippers, shrugging it off.

I am holding it in my hand, imagining you holding a weapon,
watching seals emerge from ice.

I stayed up later than you, with stacks of books and magazines,
and loud crackers—

I would stare at you in a strange fit of passion,
imagining your death,

and cry until I woke you up,

unless the snap and debris of the crackers had not
already enraged you,

and I loved you best this way:

tragically departed,

your family and I locked in mortal combat over cremation vs. burial,
all the things I wanted to tell you

poured over your grey headstone,

like the first rush of snow that kills the wreaths and flowers,
that forbids visitors,

other than those like me,

who have lain in the snow like a sled, feeling the voluptuous motions
of the earth,

who are only articulate in absence, because it cannot be betrayed,
because the first words, like the first handfuls of earth,
are barbaric, yet contained.

A measure of grass, an urn.

Everything your hand has touched, rigidity and contours I would never comprehend,
stayed in this one instance—

sleepy, your hand reaches back; still,
it reaches back.

I saw *Un Chien Andalou* and never flinched, eye injuries make one immune
to such things;

a surfeit of critical theory, also.

But I read your letters, what I could read, and felt the razor
separate my iris and pupil,

what gushes forth, not vascular: lychees in heavy syrup.

An unnatural receptiveness to horror: *they're all going to laugh at you.*

My father took me on the Scenic Railway when I was four, distracted me
by pointing out derelict toys on the roofs of the shooting galleries,

a teenage boy vomiting cotton candy by the Wild Mouse.

The fall was incidental.

You laughed at me in the letters, and I felt unwell; I felt my
father's calm,

his abiding sense of the fear that is merely apprehension; that everything
else is suspended,

where there is no time to be afraid, only to endure.

He went to Coney Island when he was very young, and got trapped on a ride
that left him, that left everyone hovering over the park for an hour.

When the machinery was fixed, they dropped them down, and yelled,
One free ride!

Dragging them back to the same, teetering height.
There are painted mermaids there, shacks simmering with deep-fried clam bellies,
the ocean.

He tried to teach me about focus. I shut down the computer where you laughed at me.

This sound, like the descent of the cars, a strange prayer, not a prayer.

These rides are rigged for our safety. The fall assimilates our play with danger;
assumes that it is not dangerous. Asking, conversely,

Look at that pink teddy bear.

Look, at the architecture of my contempt.

My father told me he liked you because you were the only man I had ever brought home
who was interested in sports.

You could talk about curling and basketball, you mentioned a squash tournament
with a semi-famous opponent.

And you had played hockey and given it up. You became interested in music, you told him.

My father should have been a blackjack dealer—he betrayed nothing, to you or me.

He was nonplussed, as he had always been, by the junkies and thieves,
the girls I brought home that now remind me of the birds he almost ran over,
and saved,

the squirrels he still names in his backyard.

These squirrels eat out of his hand; he buys grosses of peanuts, worries about the
poisoner next door.

When I returned after Christmas, I brought home a piece of equipment you wanted,
carefully wrapped and ribboned,

and you left it on the bar, half-opened: you opened it the way Frank idly noses
things on the sidewalk: dead bird, bread crusts, a single potato.

My father's knees had disintegrated. He came to see me when you left, with cartons of soup
and noodles, and we looked at the dog, and the dog looked back,

adjusting—dogs are simple.

You never thanked him, or acknowledged the many gifts, painstakingly inscribed, stupidly
expensive.

The last day, my father walked to his car and I gave him the gift, its label exposed
in a furl of silver paper.

I watched him walk to his car, limping with this small weight.

I do not think of you often. And when I do, this image supplants yours,
my father's trust and pain,

the unspoken language of gifts, how my dog pirouettes for a slice of cheese;
how you vacated me, everything—

the empty spaces where his knees were,
his trust, unspoken also, as absolute as the cards he inscribes in his unwanted responsibilities,
his hope,

that the kick is up, and it's good,

that there are no refunds, only this terrible exchange.

You keeled over in the basement, flailing, and I asked,
What, do you want me to call an ambulance?

Hurry! you said.

As you propped yourself up, you told me what to tell your family,
and I was afraid.

Your father had woken up a year before and said he felt
as though a rhinoceros was sitting on his chest.

He was in intensive care for weeks; we had unplugged the phone,
and missed the call.

The paramedics stormed through and carried you out on
a stretcher.

I followed you. To your father's hospital bed, where he looked like
a length of intubated wax;

to the IC waiting room, where we all watched episodes of *Full House*,
intently and angrily.

When he came to, he said he would prefer not to see me.
You told the paramedics you were also having a heart attack,
that would later be diagnosed as a headache.

You were undaunted: there was something on your mind, and it injured you.

To this day, I am certain that you characterize guilt as a pain
that isolates you even further—

the way the street looks in the wake of an ambulance,
fraught and empty: its lines more certain, after their fervent erasure.

I am writing poems about you, is how the small talk goes.

I call this time in my life an emotional and artistic obstacle,
as though it was an ocean, gated by black flags.

Lying is not specific to you: I love someone else.

Who is also gone—this is commonplace, and difficult.

Your grandmother's first husband's belongings: a tag, her letters.

He followed the German army into a Russian blizzard,
and died in the bottleneck.

Someone has since retrieved his belongings from a hill of snow and dirt.

You felt he had no choice and I never disagreed.

I never knew him, or you.

I am stumbling through a white haze, and I would tear my own ear off,
to liberate myself,

and I would keep moving forward, had you asked me to,
had I understood that in enduring you,

I would be splintered with ice; that I would consider falling,
leaving only a dent in the ground that ached,

incomprehensibly, with my sense of where I had been,
where I thought I was going.

Our life together had become so awful that each night,
I threw up one of the three dinners you rotated:
pasta, falafel, hot dogs in cheesy little wraps.

This passed without notice or remark.

By all rights, I should have forgotten you by now, and have,
in theory.

It is our life I cannot cross over, as though we sunk our savings
into a business that leaked money, that bled us dry,

that still represented the most terrible feelings available,
loss and hope.

What is unacknowledged, at a certain point, an invention
patented in labour and failure, somehow more valuable for this.

I think of an mulish astronaut, saying, Go ahead,
I'll catch up with you later.

I remain, caught on the scythe-end of the waning moon.

The last time we were in Vancouver,
we stayed at the Sylvia Hotel.

I took a picture of you dog-earing your book,
bleached-out, composed,

a coffee cup and pluming cigarette at your elbow.

In the direct sun that is anathema to photography,
you revealed yourself entirely,

almost indistinct from the light; one of its sheer
spokes; additionally, what is happened upon—

the fins of dolphins, breaking the water;

the orange lustre of new earth;

the short movements of a newborn squirrel, who,
in falling from its nest,

cried with grief as wasps entered its mouth; as tomcats circled—

I would never see you look like that again: in the picture, the sea-wall
seems to brace the room, the ocean shudders.

The shuddering of waves, however small,

the small, strange puling of the squirrel I drowned.

You moved a block away. In retrospect, we were separated,
but I felt like a cowboy when the town seemed to me,

not big enough for the both of us.

Your apartment an elasticized version of your room,
if enviably clear of cats and dog hair,

the masses of clothes I would hang like paintings—walking our halls in a
billow of skirts.

I think of visiting you there now, as if visiting a son at college, and admiring
his stolid collection of the four food groups, his jar of highlighters.

There was a cheap stained-glass window in the foyer, the walls were
dull pink until you stained them, and the woodwork, and the baseboards,

a muddy brown.

Everything I saw triggered memories and suspicion—

you made me tea in an unfamiliar cup and I wondered
how we were learning to renovate ourselves,

mathematically, radically—the kidney you promised to your brother,
still residing in you,

livid, insensible of your intentions, acting as two.

When I was thirteen or so, it seemed clear to me that I would never
have a boyfriend.

I was too ugly, too strange, and I let that hemlock pass
through me, as truth.

As it turned out, I would spend most of my life yelling
at a chorus of men for leaving their socks on the floor,

like mice or vomit, like a trail of crumbs.

You never left a single sock at large; you balled them together,
heel to toe, stacked them in the designated drawer.

I feel I am on the verge of understanding what transpired between us,
when I think of these socks, nestled in their black bouquets.

It has to do with the difference between entropy and action,

perpetual motions, performed by people, who, in their constant yelling,
compose a play.

In this play, the man and woman argue and walk into a garden.
The roses are opening, unfurling themselves.

The petals detaching: I am standing in our bedroom, wrenching out your drawer,
and filling the floor with these dark blossoms.

I walk through them barefoot and they are soft, and they are distressed;
they snap with electricity.

I want to unravel them with needles, restore them.

I had my own room, though it remained unlocked and open:
I had nothing to hide.

You would barge in and out, asking where the can-opener was,
what was I doing, who gave you that?

I stopped keeping a diary shortly after we met.

I could not have explained to myself, how I had learned to detach longing
and its function,

that I betrayed you always and never,

that I had learned to think like a criminal, locating deviance
in escape,

and marking the days.

You were responsible, but I was culpable.

I would wait for you to sleep, and the second you snored,
or even breathed erratically, I exiled you to the couch,

lying lengthwise in your absence, limpid.

The times you went out, I felt like a latchkey adolescent,
content in my mess and intrigues,

pushing the stereo dial past 3, revelling in a past that was
surely lost.

I had no idea how quickly you were moving into this past,
like a fugitive tachyon,

an ace in a sleeve.

That it would be a year before it occurred to me to fall into bed without walking
tentatively to my far side,

before I would stop waiting to hear you, before this waiting
opened me,

and I recognized everywhere I have lived—

in single rooms and basements, beside your drowsing head,

as you roiled with your own dreams, as you waited, to be excused.

The street where I live is garish with Christmas,
a bright carnival, each light or wreath a code

for unseen interiors.

This evening, in the blink of red and green,

I am thinking of our tiny tree, its boughs canting with the ornaments
your parents gave us, glass ovals in slotted boxes,

the miniature white lights you strung to its base.

On our last Christmas together, I bought you ten presents,
each one leaden with nostalgia, largesse—

a vintage hockey game with metal opponents, a digital video camera,
Parisian teapot, KISS box set, Frank's baby tooth set in platinum,

a photograph of the site of our first kiss, in King's College
Circle,

beneath the shadow of the CN Tower.

Every exposure distorted, as though the tower was being attacked,
its apex erased by spears and circles.

I framed the most distorted of these, thinking it represented
what had always been wrong, and right,

and you thanked me, and you hung it above your desk.

You sat at this desk, composing lovesick letters, to a woman I have
never met—

she is small and fair-haired; she fed you chocolate and wondered
how it is one gets along in this world.

Your answers were practical; I want to tell her, now, that it is a matter of moving
forward,

before getting caught.

I want to see her walk past me in these green and red vapours,
and stop, staggered by the glare of what is evident—

the eventual gauntlet of dead pines and lustrous trash; how we celebrate
what has died as though this birth, or that birth,

may end differently.

Yesterday, I found the last of my macabre souvenirs.

A snow-shaker with a double-sided image of you as a boy and man,
a Bay box containing a golden heart.

Your mother worked hard, selling suits and coating her home in ammonia;
the heart was a tasteless and touching memento,

the snowy images so appalling, I continue to look for a suitable burial place.

I intended to throw it into the Gulf of Mexico,
and worried, at the thought of a child being obscurely injured.

The necklace—

When I was a teenager, I bought a record at a garage sale. Two Catskills
comedians, photographed sitting on a lawn, on toilets.

One fat, one skinny, their material racy for the time.
The skinny comedian was the straight man and he censured the fat one
for his vulgar observations about Spanish fly and Saran Wrap.

Like most lost things, I miss this recording, miss the pathetic audacity.

I would like to give the comedians the pendant, the pictures,
and tell them I remember them, the name of their record,

and ask them to return these objects, and, as their record title suggested,
ask them to say, *Take Your Love and Shove It Up Your Heart.*

This Christmas, I leashed Frank and fled my parents' house in Pointe Claire,
walked him by the United Church creche: four plywood pieties painted
by Hazel Henry, in 1959.

Two wise men, a bashful Mary, and Jesus, unperturbed at their feet.

We walked past Marina Crescent, where two snowmen stood, one fallen, one
tilting; the elementary school, its windows a tablature of the idea of snow

and snowflakes, blind with battered paper.

I tasted white glue, the tang of dull, industrious blades. Saw a father teaching
his children to ski; as Frank ploughed through the drifts, he called out,

Raise your poles and keep your feet pointed.

The walls were lashed with ivy and puckered orange leaves; the fire hydrants
lining the curb were a livid, paintbox red.

The father sailed through the snow as his children stepped like frogs, and I
remembered

visiting my parents' friends, who had a daughter my age, five or so.

Her parents trundled us into the car one morning and took us to a sports store
where they carefully chose and bought gear,

and I assumed I would be outfitted too.

We drove to a clearing, and everyone stepped out and started to ski,
making slight, determined tracks,

and I sat in the backseat as the mother chain-smoked and stared into the distance,
she and I sat there for hours,

both of us resigned, still as pieces of paper, a field of new snow;
as they cut past and through us.

An old man passed us on a walker, and Frank began to bark.
And I remarked on his blue eyes—

he looked mildly concerned,

but his eyes were the whole synoptic, the blue sky, heavy with vapours,
blue treacherous ice; the blue wooden vestments;

the blue glove in the snowbank I considered slipping on,
and passed by.

The relief of blue veins on my bare hands,
somewhere, churning near me,

the hypnotic blue of the lake, discarded as the
night lurched into black.

On and off during the holidays, someone called
and hung up, many times.

The name seemed familiar, and I thought about it as I unpacked
my bags, and called the number.

The message is garbled, it sounds like the woman is speaking through
a blizzard, and I realized it was the name of the astrologer,

that shutterbug you fell asleep to (*and then she woke me up*).

Your other girlfriend called me also, at three in the morning,
last fall. Hung up, three times.

These women do not want to apologize or make amends.
I am a complaint department to them. A Formica counter
that they can lean on, vexed and somewhat afraid

of their own audacity.

The instructions are complicated and translated from Aramaic
into English, then Plutonian.

Larceny and charges are involved, a colour-coded wire-board
and nautical terminology.

I just wanted a boyfriend, they might say. This is supposed to be simple.

I would nod my assent as they opened and closed their throats.

As fragile and voracious as hatchlings—

I dreamed about them both, the second in particular.
Her teeth bared, as flat and cheerless as piano keys.

She is drinking from your mother's purple decanter,
offering me a seat at an event you are presiding over,

in Saskatoon.

I slap her as hard as I can, and she still smiles.

I warn you—I am starting to like her.

Her body deflating, as if filled with hard, shifting beans;
her skin stretching in various accommodations,

your privacy and pride

absenting her as she reaches for the glass, the light, the telephone, almost
mistaking me

for a friend.

Similar dreams recur, a recrudescent impulse to batter her,
her imperviousness a constant.

It is like slapping clay; we are complicit.

She may watch over you also, examining the motility of your heart.

She may sleep like a stone, possessed of certainties I have never
had: the oyster yielding its pearl

after ceaseless irritation; the way a spoon thickens in measures of liquid;
how the sun lit you up in pieces,

irradiating the moon's brooding—

how it dashed against the window, how the glass admitted its entry,
without breaking: your whole body is lucent,

moving through me in tides.

The pain is in abeyance, generally.

Asserting itself in a language I do not understand:
the sounds that animals make when they are injured.

Wolves that circle each other, howling
for something lost, or close at hand.

I made you say it until the words collapsed,
I am never coming back.

I lost my way, long before you.

My friend's baby spits out a tofu hotdog and screams
Fix it!

I am jamming my head through the slats of a crib,
wailing this way,

why have you left me.

Swallowing hard as life seems to slip through the woods
pursuing and eluding me.

Its taste in my mouth: what I know has changed.

We met at a motel by the water, the first night.

Exchanged presents, a mouldering Selected Byron,
a tiny seahorse: the name of the place.

You told me they mated for life. Later, we would go to
the Waverley,

and listen to the pimps on payphones, screaming;

unclutching to visit the washroom, shivering below
its banners of blood.

The wastebasket would fill with Trojans,
the walls would spread in fissures, shake.

Later we would grapple in washrooms, stairwells,
the banquette of a Portuguese nightclub.

Our deception an armada.

For seven years, we looked back with false sentiment at the site
of our departure,

as though we had set sail in this red tide, holding up our hands,
lashing up two anchors,

until they corroded.

He cried at my calumny. She still does: we also left marks.

Others were determined to expose you
as hateful, and untrue.

A friend told me you walked her to the streetcar,
kissed her goodbye.

On the lips.

This seemed more reasonable to me than her,
she had been a hooker and her sense of obscenity

was as sharp as the secrets you swallowed.

Long swords, the hilt is a smile, the hilt is an abject curve,

turning in and out of what you want and what you know:
the taste of steel, what emerges from its perforations.

My sister snores like a chainsaw: I had no idea. My mother screams,
in ten-minute intervals, and my father mutters imprecations.

I cannot sleep near them; it is not the noise.

It is what is entrusted in my hearing this chaos. An irregular heartbeat,
unacknowledged infirmities, sheer terror.

My brother has sleep apnea; my best friend sleeps with a cup, in case
she vomits and chokes—

I have been alone too long now. I cannot hover, as I did,
around such frail concessions,

your ragged breath and rapid movements—

making torrid admissions, that it was too hard in spite of,
because of, my close attention.

When the dreams, I mean visions, became unbearable,
I visited the boy's grave.

He was buried in Whitby in a cemetery pushed back by housing
developments until the graves looked like sardines packed tight,

sealed with stone.

His was the only bare plot: the others were identically dressed in
bright plastic wreaths,

as though he was being snubbed at a carnival; as though he had
refused to participate,

as always,

lurking outside of the school dances, dealing hash,
skipping the grad photos,

walking through the halls with his head bent low, a baseball cap
shadowing his face.

His cold diffidence astonished me,

astonishes me: I left three bunches of tulips he would have despised,
and when you left, he left me too.

I was sure I had not displaced my fears in him,

fears that would spread as tulips do, as they unfold themselves
and tear into such certainties,

ending where they began—

Today as I drive past Whitby I see his initials on a stone escarpment;
a sign that says KEEP YOUR DISTANCE.

Other signs, that I keep to myself. He hated my attention, turned
away from it;

he turned to it also, like a fibrous petal, extended towards
the sun,

the way I will still blaze, remembering him; the way he will suffer this—

my hands are rough with pollen, and I held him once as I held you and he wished,
he wishes I would step back,

and move forward; he is graceful and still, steadies me.

i miss you and our boy.

This is one of your emails, in part, sent some time before you would lose
the lower cases, all references to "our boy."

You were unfailingly kind to me,

repressing your objections and exhaustion: as a child I suffered from nosebleeds,
remember sitting in foyers and cloak rooms,

swallowing blood.

I was taken to a doctor, and this ended; this ended when you contemplated our life
and retrieved a cautery,

searing the connective tissue; making sense.

Do not imagine drowning in blood, a friend wrote.

In our bedroom, red curtains, pillows, a lavish mink-tailed blanket.
In the spaces you left,

lights flared—the scene of an accident, the arc of red lights picking
out bloodshed.

Sweeping over and past what emerges: a man with his head in his hands,
a woman slumped in the wreckage with her boy.

Their bodies, on impact, shatter the windshield, and it radiates like a plan.

The email's subject heading is My Angel.

You knew that one of us would have to go.

Among my many and grievous charges: that I would never see Paris,
that I would be the woman in the Marianne Faithfull song,

who looks at her life like a choke-chain, and falls.

Three years ago, you took me there.
We are incredulous in every picture, strangely relaxed.

My parents won a trip in the 1970s and toured Europe,
returning with photographs I continue to covet and love —

my mother, her hair permed into a huge Afro, standing stiffly
in front of the Eiffel Tower;

my father, with his ubiquitous cigarillo, posing likewise
before the Prado, an abject gondolier.

Our photographs are similar, suggesting seizure, little claims.

We saw everything it seems, retaining very little.

Your presence among the hibiscus and black iron gates;
the stone banks of the gray river, where the pigeons converged.

I would wake long before you, watch yellow-suited
men hose the streets and wait,

until our coffee tray arrived, until the day cracked
and we persisted and wondered,

at Cézanne's hunger, in a plush red banquette,
in the zoo,

where one lion emerged, boxed in a tiny enclosure,
roaring with a sadness so acute

I could not leave it behind.

This creature's anguish was simple, like mine, like yours.

An insistent recollection, of a country large enough to inhabit,
where one's nature is pedestrian,

one's need to serve, while tracking the metallic thrill of fresh
kills, infinite expanses of leisure,

one's thinned but essential pride.

A friend made us a quilt, using a hearth pattern.

Tumultuously coloured, from a green batik to pale yellow calico,
bordered, definitively, in red.

A heart in the middle, cut from her dead budgie's blanket.

The bird would stomp around on this silk square,
beak it into a ball, vomit on it as if feeding a baby.

I was talking about our hamster to someone
who said, of her own bird,

that it was the size of her heart.

The quilt is folded up, and never used.

It says nothing about us, biting on the bars,
there is only her perspective—

from a great height, how small we are.

This little woman I saw at the hospital,
eighty or so in a green coat and alligator T-strap shoes,

all of her belongings in Ziploc bags.

As slow as muddy water, gathering her forms, pleating them.
And when she dropped a packet, I bolted up to retrieve it.

She has long, platinum hair and glassine skin.

She thanked me, as she has her entire life, as her beauty has arrested
everyone and time—

I called you from this same hospital, two years ago.
Speaking quickly, in tears. Come home, you said.

This is all I remember: I must have rushed back, as I am
rushed back to this thought,

and envying her certain passage.

I want to come home.

We read *A Moveable Feast* together;
recently, I was able to look through it again.

I wrote you that I had thought of you
at the last page, cried.

You said you had done the same, last fall.

Take care of yourself, you wrote.

He and Hadley are together, and long since separated.

The verbs are like eels.

The pain is similar, an electrical fusion
between intention and innocence.

— *when we were poor and very happy.*

The tenses coil uncertainly, unsure of their reach.

I want to be happy, you said.

I saw a picture of you the other day, your eyes are sodden dirt.

We have both become enormous, people talk.
We are heavy with consequence—

like gas-filled corpses, or bloated bags of evidence
emerging from the skin of a lake.

I see you loaded with groceries, laundry, magazines.

Someone I dated briefly who said he wanted to ask women
what they wanted,

to write these things down, and get it done.

Writing about you is like hurrying through the litany
before confession proper.

Taking a Gravol before a trip, waiting one hour to enter the water,
priming a canvas,

lacing skates before a game.

The snow-shaker is now empty: one fast smash and the floor
was alight with water and flakes.

It is sitting on my counter like a plain signal: I think of Howard Hughes
collecting his fingernails and skin.

The adult picture means nothing to me, your smile is forced and fatuous.

The little boy is truly smiling, in his too-girlish white frock, among
his empire of blocks.

I have nothing against him, though I feel he has something against me.

Latent and related to his hair that falls in pretty ringlets,
a complex relationship to affection he is earning as he builds

walls and towers,

an unyielding will to escape these very structures, in a tantrum
of kicks and heaving;

heaving, you began to speak and blocked out my past.

I continue to confuse every man with you, and wonder if your wife
counters,

weighing your mysteries against the tiny anchor of her diamond,
cataleptic with disbelief.

Alone again, this season, I wonder how you could have left me in the snow,
the snow that made me shrink further, that shut me inside.

We were always alone together. But you made yourself a pocket
in the drift, where we both retreated.

I have lost someone else. I do not know who he is anymore:
the cold is relentless—

hazardous paths, bleak perspectives,
air entering like an incision.

I am a liar also, will not tell the truth about what transpired
between us. I can only allude to the most grotesque

articles, the spikes of the fever.

I am cramped in our bathroom with a plastic bag on my head,
which you arrogate and claim,

like a mother with her child's urine-soaked sheets,
you run outside and scream about where I belong.

A mental institution, similar stations.

It is cold and I ask you to come inside. The neighbours drink
in this quarrel, like cats and cream.

I knew you did not love me anymore, that was all I could say,
and did not.

Your story was better. I was slowly coming apart, without
reason,

she tried to kill herself again today!
You do not need this in your life.

Advice is easy: the oxygen advised me also that it was leaving,
that I might not miss its mere alacrity.

You had called 911 before. And felt like Judas, you said,
for doing so.

Our roles reversed, you were the angry Jesus who is tired of multiplying; tired of his job.

And I was Judas, the first suicide, who felt compelled to speak out,
that whatever was happening was wrong,

because it was premeditated, because no one bothered to let him know.

The moment we let someone enter our lives, they come equipped
with enough ammunition to destroy us,

though the terms of destruction are unclear.

Looking back, it was not as much the lying, but that you laughed
at me, because I had not caught on.

Mistaking trust for stupidity, old failures:
The igloo has no door, it's ridiculous.

I am thinking of welding cubes together with white sugar,
closing in the structure.

Wolves pass in packs, the floor is dense with fur and smoke—
it is warm inside, and safe.

Yesterday, a dead grackle in the hedge, blood.

This morning, a mouse on the carpet, a single puncture hole.

A stone and a cross mark each homicide,
starting a map that encloses what is fluid in a grid.

Extending a key:

fixed numerals: the succession of time,
marked in thirds,

like a common clover, three playing cards.

I will always be alone, in this strange river, that changes as I change it,
shifting the rocks and silt.

Fish rustle past. Cutting the water, traversing its shifting depths.

You were stupid with beauty, a wordless blazon,

your hair shot through with violet,

eyes like black dahlias in milk, your mouth crepe
myrtle.

The way you looked through windows, as if looking for light.

In the end, the bloom had waned into dusk—

the dark mechanics of the flower, that flowers show,
as they muddy the water, and wanting an element,

gather, and let go.

You were wearing a black puffy coat: its sleeves barely reached your wrists;
you were unshaven, the colour of clay.

I asked you where you bought the coat.

At a store called Great Stuff. Well, they will have to change the name, I said.

You declined to walk Frank as it was drizzling outside,

and that is the last time I saw you.

I spent New Year's alone, contemplating my inability to concentrate.

I watched balls drop in three cities, men and women in red hats holding
red balloons,

commercials for liability lawyers, unredressed disabilities, peerless
diamonds, set in fat, gold bands.

I made five resolutions and broke them all this morning.

The last New Year's we spent together, I had a migraine and my brother visited,
still alone. We drank champagne and you had ginger-ale,

there were Cheesies and Ruffles.

My brother left at midnight. Later, he would remark on how many times
you had left to check your email: I hadn't noticed.

A salesman whose outlet is located on Orfus Road hawking suits,
cautioned revellers, Be careful, be careful.

The crowds fit together like cell nuclei, and counted down the seconds
until another year passed,

leaving me somewhere in between,

the sound of your steps on the stairs, tearing away;
the voice of the suit-man,

unpracticed, genuinely ill at ease.

One of your notes, discovered in a box,
a pleated triangle,

you had torn the edge off a sheet of paper,
apologized about something.

I am always apologizing, you said.

Also in the box: a vial of dispenser cologne,
Obsession for Men,

our first artefact: I have forgotten its significance,
the significance of your regrets,

their pattern—like a man applying cologne, habitually.
Oblivious to its own premise—

my dog rolling in grass,
erasing his trail:

all of what he has forgotten and learned.

The night before, a friend visited, and spent the night.

He patted my head and told me how to say What a beautiful fat baby,
in Mandarin.

He slept on the couch; I heard him pacing in the morning,
anxious to be let out.

I do not know how I became this way.

His eyes curved like mandibles. I told him that when I first
moved here,

I walked by a street-corner that was strewn with
twenty chicken heads.

I unlocked the door and returned to bed, knowing we would
never speak again.

I had let him see too much. In doing so, he became disgusting to me.

The hindquarters of the squirrel I saw this morning,
rotting in a hedge.

The tangle of his blankets, other evidence of his sleepless
night: a glass, books, a pillow mashed into quarters.

The Korean girls are dressed in jewelled pink robes,
broken bottles roll through the gutters,

among the usual and unusual debris.

There is a drawing on my lawn. On a church donation
envelope.

Three trees, staggered.

The third appears to be in flames.

Nothing seems to change, but the imperiousness of fate.
Pears, apples.

Indolent death, dragging its scythe across the grass,
marking it with ribbons, tinsel, and paper plates—

signs that are barely evident, sickening still.

An empty envelope, scribbled on by someone who knows better;
who in knowing, will not pony up.

The psychic was sweetly overweight, like a miscalculated flan,
and visibly trembling.

One of the party guests was loud and disorderly, and the psychic
compulsively cleansed his aura,

and arranged my cards into a cross.

I have no interest in the occult, but he looked, among
the fashionable gathering,

like a boy who used to walk away from my school bus, hitching up
his polyester pants as we shrieked from the back window.

He asked what I wanted to know, and I told him you and I were
looking for a house. That I wasn't sure where we would go.

He turned over the rest of the Major Arcana in a row,
and blanched.

We had been talking about writing, and felt content—

he wore pentacle necklaces over a brown turtleneck and liked
poems about rocks and arrowheads.

You are going. To need. To.
Clear out some dead wood, he said, in little fits.

Then abruptly stopped, waving off my money,
stuffing my number in his pocket like a loose thread.

I had no idea he meant you.

I had stopped keeping diaries, because of their sameness,
their false authenticity,

like the worthless, gorgeous stamps from Trinidad and Tobago
I used to send away for, and paste in albums.

Janet gave me a leather-bound book, some time before.

The writing starts without reason, circles and reverses on the pages,
like a skittish horse, its mane plaited for show.

There are photographs of our last Christmas, short editorials
about the same.

Their apparency is horrifying—the writing shrinks from it in
rough waves.

My grey face, bloated and cheerless; your entire body, torquing
away from gifts that must have felt like anaphylaxis,

like a wire mother in a cage, Monkey (another of my names for you).

We used to hang lights and deck a little tree. This year, you tossed a
wooden fishing lure I had given you into a bowl, hooking it.

I have no idea what you gave me. In the pictures, you are wearing
a tiara and I am squished somewhere nearby,

surrounded with silver paper,

handing you another reason and another, to abdicate
what we had, and abjure it entirely.

The Polaroids remain in the locked box; its keys locked elsewhere:
such complicated intimacy.

They pre-date you, and have been winnowed down to a select
group, that flatter me and no one else.

You outnumber the rest: you loved to be photographed.

What I had thought was personal was something different, to you.

In one shot, you offer yourself like a hit of coke: you are a line
of white heat, cut in the first thrall of acquisition.

The rest is always diminishment and contrition:
this body turning away; my part in this gesture.

Andrew, one of the men who lived upstairs, had a girlfriend,
all blonde hair, black lip-liner and roller blades.

They would screw in the kitchen and her screams would leak
through the windows and hover, like hot air.

You pulled me to the side of the house to listen, and I realized
you were madly excited.

I was only curious. You would speak about her to your girlfriend,
like a *Penthouse* Letter.

Her moaning lines the box that I never open.

Arousal remembered as the complex circuitry that renders
communication possible; that falsifies it, at once.

My aunt was telling me about putting her dog to sleep,
as the rest of the family assembled and reassembled themselves

in the few, hard-backed chairs.

I had to leave the room. I am not myself these days, I said.

She repeated this to anyone who asked where I was: there was a certain
dramatic resonance; better, it fit

with how I looked and how I acted, like a soap opera stand-in:
Today, the role of Victor Newman will be performed by—

The next day was the same, and the next.

I cry so much, I fail to notice. Occasionally, one eye or the other
becomes infected, magnifies,

how easy it is to disassemble, beyond repair.

To lie down in one's failure, as if retiring to a tartan blanket,
a selection of chew-toys.

And accept the needle with the tears. Whatever it is they are crying
about does not concern you.

It is something else, the days you spent chasing your tail;
missing and catching it,

completing the circle you trundle towards now,
enervated and empty, as warm there as earth, as grass,

as everything new that is changed by, that encloses our grief.

When you left, I thought for some time that I was a zombie, living a life
I had imagined, not living at all.

Lately, I considered someone leaving, crying out, Don't leave me.
Not knowing who I am talking to.

Snow is expected in the next few days. It will cover the trees in the parkette,
where in divining signs *I miss everything*,

where the trees have been switchbladed, parsed into stakes,
and shudder.

My sympathy is misplaced. Because I am not myself these days,
it does not recognize me.

I hate to sleep, and postpone it because it is a serviceable filling
between two slices of green bread,

a sigh between sieges,

stupidly hopeful in its assertions: that there is another world. Its geography
is bare and comforting,

one strip mall, an apartment that overlooks water.

Other, insistent details. Vengeance and love, making farce entrances,
lingering, briefly, like certainties

when morning attacks.

I have lured myself to sleep for so long, with practical delusions.

In time, all will be revealed—my pillow sheets twist into slips of paper,
as devised by the Far East Fortune Cookie Company.

You and I once ordered dinner from Ho-Lee-Chow, and you snapped our cookie.
It said, You like Chinese food.

I am envying your sleep tonight, as I always did.

You are a newlywed, the barn slopes with possibilities.

I am peering through the slats of a truck, shank to shank
with everyone who has mistaken their life for a prelude

to something other than a room of men in bloody aprons,
prodding us forward, the odd one murmuring, I know, I know.

— is a fresh, lively and accomplished piece—and it was on our short list—but it lacks a certain narrative thrust.

Rejection is stunning when it glances the truth,

of who you suspect you may be, may appear to be, in spite of your best efforts to modify these perceptions.

For example, I write poems I would not like to read, and am not alone in this opinion.

My Indonesian visitor referred to this, combatively, as a failure to communicate. Others take a pass, like I do with everything from Smollett to Tolkien.

Not for me.

I am needy and selfish, intermittently destructive.

The narrative is tragic, but static; ephemeral in the manner of a bad commercial for bad shoes;

a fever chart that spikes like a picket fence,

the heat in tropical climates, the glacial slopes of Baffin Island.

You said I was unhappy and did not lie. There were worse things you might have said.

That I reminded you of the vomit I walked over, recently. Hefty with nutrients, wretched with remorse.

Yours and mine, as disparate as the bilious puddle, its hearty constituents.

One of the last times we spoke, you told me you
had arranged a big party for your father's birthday.

By your lugubrious account, it had been a disaster.

Your mother choking on a ham hock, your father
receiving three identical gifts of the Titanic in a bottle.

Your grandmother pitched down a flight of stairs.

I felt no sympathy, thought, Of course, of course.

If I am unhappy, you are envious. This emotion is Park Place and Boardwalk
to you,

the site of hotels that never materialize.

The dice in your palm, tumbling like brittle bones,
declaiming that defeat is inevitable;

that the game is crooked;

that your life is an Orion of accidents that hunt you down,
metal traps or snares,

your grandmother's mechanical argument, that perfection had no place there.

You refuse and despise these errors and they cleave to you.

I was following your mother around her kitchen, trying to help.
Wiping the counter, refolding the gingham tea towels.

Have you tried this new Swiffer thing, she asked, and the intimacy of the
question disarmed me.

I was sorting through five different answers as she said, With that place,
it's not likely to make a difference.

I stood there pleating the oven-skirt. I had pursued vast tumbleweeds of cat hair,
gathered beetle husks that piled up like fish in a creel.

Making little inroads with each push—

Each carpeted stair plumped as I walked back to the basement,
as I imagined her running her fingers over me,

her white gloves coming away dirty, the corners of her mouth
turning down like a dustpan.

She would sit on the edge of the couch, drinking wine
until her tongue tripped.

Her casual wear starched, the limpid pink and white florals
as alert as botanical diagrams.

Her legs crossed, occasionally flashing the ankle bracelet
she wore under pantyhose.

And as her voice seeped into molasses, I would watch the motion
of this golden band,

that was as exotic as a feather-fringed peignoir, more so,
for its secrecy.

I thought of her creeping through the house at midnight,
the bracelet's small clamour a faint rebuke,

her ankles reliefed in the moonlight, wild fauns.

In the funeral parlour, your grandfather's casket hugging the far wall,
your grandmother, his second wife,

alone in the corner, hissing at the first family:
the barbarous thieves.

They come into my house and lift the floorboards,
she said. Slit the mattresses, toss the rooms.

Across the street, their elderly associate watches with a spyglass,
I leave the blinds drawn.

Your mother and I stood together as your great-aunt entered,
in knee socks, an apron and gumboots,

a fringe of white hair on her Popeye chin.

She tilted towards the casket, and suddenly, drifted away,

and we excused ourselves and walked the perimeter of the
parking lot, laughing ourselves sick.

There had been hardships in his life, more remained:
your grandmother's little hands like the hooks she sewed into bodices,

the points of her needles, how she blinded herself with silver darts.

Your mother's face heavy with this and other sorrows, this one time,
smooth, opening like a lily,

she was more beautiful than that—drawing me next to her in the cold,
her breath visible,

I held on to her like a ribbon, and we coiled back and forth.

Press this between the stiffness of what I do not care to read into
anymore,

a difficult story, that, when shaken, releases her fragrance,
the shape of her beauty—

the earth breaking into pieces, as it begins to receive the dead.

Time alone is biased: it is what everyone craves,
what they dread.

It fosters eccentricities, erases subtle lines between civility
and villainy.

If you are not attentive, you may start wearing tea cozies,
and telling the operator that you don't care if your swearing makes her uncomfortable:

I am not your child.

Make paella with lychees and tissue paper,

break any plate that even suggests a dinner for two.

It is exhilarating, and unnerving: you will find yourself speaking
out loud:

Would it kill you to run a brush through your hair?
The worst criminals understand this, and organize their cells
like beehives,

taming ants and shelving their books according to height,
weight, colour, and content.

Prisons are like operating theatres, in their regimens and order.

Inhabited by men and women who understand that freedom
is a compulsion first,

secondly, an impassive assault, a twister that insists
we salvage and secure

what little we have—

in the hurricane's whip-tail, we see ourselves,
and recoil. We cannot be helped;

knowing this propels us to save ourselves—

drawings in caves, that seem to articulate the distance
between limits known and imagined—

imagined as a red tiger, imagined as its seething blood.

During our summer tryst, it became obvious we still
loved each other,

that we could never be together.

I thought of our first terms, that there would be no trips
to Ikea, no parents,

that we would take holidays as an opportunity to kill ourselves
somewhere exotic; that we live on lemons and ice,

visit no one but the vault of stars beyond the balcony.

I continued to hesitate. You met me at a tavern by Coach House
Press, wearing a purple vest grommeted with tiny mirrors.

Spilled your drink, from your mouth to the table, and I grabbed
a bar rag, and smiled.

At your embarrassment, your frangible pride.

In the subway, you, as always, grabbed me and ran away,
yelling that you loved me.

This time, I stood there and took it.

I absorbed it, and wrung out its many promises,

like the dirty bar rag, I changed shape as you went east,
and I went west,

towards a new frontier, filled with purple sage and black riders,

the saloon you intended to occupy until I, the hardened server,
decided to ply you with whiskey and sharp pinches;

and with a spin of my skirt,
I would reveal petticoat after petticoat,

progressively threadbare, as tender as an artichoke,
submitting its heart.

If you are an obstacle, I have been blessed.

The lightning that stays movement; the diligence of certain people's
touch, how it disarms you,

inscribes your flesh like a scar.

My mother touched my face this Christmas, and I could not speak
or move as her hand drew and quartered me.

It is not that I wasted my life with you; it is the way in which the end
ruined everything.

Like the choirboys who praised the Virgin on Valentine's Day,
before having their throats slit, other prayers.

That you may have been blocking other impulses, mine,
yours,

to cross at red lights; to spear a bagel from a plugged-in toaster,
with a fork.

To become infirm and miss the sound of the chorus,

Et in hora mortis nostrae (× 3)
　　　　　　Ave Maria.

As you take up the knife,
you fixate on a silence that prohibits orisons, the clamour of grace.

A man followed me home the other night, his eyes
streaming with Mace; he was extremely agitated, and looking to fight.

He made several unintelligible threats, a few that were direct and pointed.

Before he got to my house, I stopped.

We have both had bad nights, I said. Please don't be angry.

He told me if a star fell from the skies it would look like me,
and wandered away.

There are so many men in my life, I have lost count. I never see them,
but apprehend their presence.

A phalanx of angels; convicts in leg-irons, making tracks.

The heart's obscenity is anatomical. If I were a mad scientist,
I would turn this organ into a honeycomb—

each ventricle would contain its honey and stings,
the drone of its many correlatives,

preparing itself to be abandoned by the itinerant swarm,
and its little aches,

its bristling tenancy.

Our loyalties divided, friends took sides.

Several of them had access to certain information,
our vicious fights and discontent.

Trust is a scarecrow, a safe word, a low whistle in the dark.

It is like seeing your mother in curlers and face cream; ideally, it is
like marvelling at her, later.

You kept me in the wire rollers and green mask.

It began with a painful admission. She has problems.

This took shape like a head of spiral curls,
exposed me, reddened and raw.

In bad dreams, women open their doors to party guests in laddered hose
and a house dress.

They open their doors to admissions they are not a party to,
as they vault into the bathroom,

drawing familiar lines and filling intervals as the guests circle,

waiting for you to appear, with a tray of shrimp puffs; in an aurora of Joy;
your problems dimmed, as hot as the tea lights you lined

across the mantel,

because you are eccentric; because this characteristic can be chic
or scary—

you start tossing appetizers like chum, and shiver,
knowing that their problems no longer concern you.

They are nothing but hunger: you are getting in their way.

You married her, and I wanted to ask you why,
although I assumed you disliked prohibitive rents, other bills,

the isolation of your misery.

I think of you crying during the ceremony,
discreetly.

Baroque chandelier crystals, pearls on hemlines.

You have wasted most of your life's sorrow,
stolen and misapprehended it.
Occupying other's miseries like rented tuxedos—

you shoot your cuffs as she short-steps the aisle,
and her face is flushed, and modest.

Two tears trembling there, like cubic zirconia;
like the glass that will always separate you,

little groom, sloping into the cake,
its lyrical rosettes,

staking the white layers,

that are as prim as the detachable tags that, with a single flourish,
separate the living and the dead.

I think about our wedding; think that it happened often,
and without ceremony.

The day I met your family, and clomped through the house
so loudly, the figurines of shepherds and shepherdesses shook,

and your mother shook, her hands rabid with dish soap,

and your sister-in-law shook her hair into her eyes,

and the warm beer shook in its crates.

The men were superfluous.

The day your mother let me wash a dish was our honeymoon.

The day your father asked if I were perhaps from Wales;
the night your brother turned into the crook of my arm—

every day you rushed home to me, without stopping.

The bells sounded, and the streets filled with rice
as white as my shoes, picking through it,

leaving faint shapes.

I never slept, would listen to the things you said in your sleep
like "sombrero" or "that is not my shoe."

Watched your eyes drift like fish under your lids,
the reeds of your lashes,

how your hair waved in little Kahunas; the way you smelled,
like cling peaches; how you moved your feet

like a monkey on a vine.

Let you steal all the blankets and make a bindle,
unfold them as you protested, snapping "dovetail,"

or "monster truck."

And I would resume watching you, as you sank into sleep.

The moon would fill the window, falling too.

I have not seen this light since; I am content to let it follow you.

We drove into Niagara Falls at noon, with "The Future" blaring,
you looking slick at the wheel.

Rented a room in a motel with a trapezoidal pool,
and visited every haunted house and wax museum on the strip.

We went to a maze, and got lost. Stood there, mystified, until
I lifted the canvas, and, cheating, got us out of there.

We did not see the Falls at midnight, we were otherwise
occupied.

The bed was pita-shaped and we rolled from either edge like
chickpeas.

Nothing could stand in our way, even if we had seen the future,

we would have gathered closer;

Things are going to slide, slide in all directions.

How the neon of the strip blazes and stops;

it is electrifying, to refuse thought.

I am standing at the airport bar in Texas with you,
reaching for a cold beer.

We are on our way to New Mexico: the beer is cold,
the best I ever had.

When we visited the Rio Grande gorge and left our initials there,
among innumerable others,

above the thread of the river, the car, shattered on the rocks.

I look at names in trees and stone differently now. As if they are
extras in an old movie, everything but their ambition dead.

A ranch-hand passing a rope and a filly to John Wayne.

Hurtling to his end, either proud or ashamed of this slender claim:
I was there. I met him. He seemed very nice.

This is the kind of shadow cast by stones; this is the way the river looks,
from a great distance;

Large enough to fall into, and drown.

I am teaching one of your books, and as my students cite you,
I invent mean anagrams or homonyms,

my face expressionless.

When they talk I think about poetry's occasional incredulity.

It rarely varies and is expressed as follows:

How could this have happened?

The writer is usually referring to loss, the universe's refusal to bend
accordingly.

I was washing a cupboard with an old toothbrush the night you first
slept with her. Something like that.

Tonight, an entire shelf of dishes fell on my head when I thought of you.

And I thought, that is more like it. I was stunned, and pirated;
there will be shards on the floor for months,

lying in wait, more piercing in their semblance to the form
they adopted, briefly,

before falling apart.

The owner of my local received sweaters and French cuff shirts
for Christmas. He had asked for a train set.

My wife hates my clothes, wants me look different, he said.
Why do women do this?

I thought of all of my friends, buying pink shirts and turtlenecks
last December,

of myself, balling up your leather jacket and kafalah scarf,
and, over time, building you a new wardrobe.

I should have let you be:

recently, my father spoke furiously about gifts of clothing,
felt that he was being dressed like a little doll.

My doll, after chrysalis.

Spreading your fiery wings and lighting out,

dressed like me, by me.

Your wife once told someone she loved me.

When I was a child, my friends always tried to steal my dolls.

You used to spend what seemed like hours in the bathroom,
in that slanted, fungus-breeding rectangle.

What are you doing in there, I would ask.
This sort of recollection makes me understand your departure better.

There was a paucity of evidence: tissue paper torn at the corner,
my manicure scissors transferred, from the cabinet to the sink.

The lighting was garish and unforgiving.

I would wonder if you looked at yourself with hatred, or love.

If the tissue-ends were milagros, of some kind.

Cut into prayers, the shape of your new life:

a soft and pliable woman,

who would never abrade you with her attention;
with a scrutiny as pitiless as the light of that weird basilica.

Your silence speaks to convictions I will never apprehend,
to the covenants between men and women

that function like a register.

Toaster oven, pillow shams, never speak of her again.

I will be absent from your poems, my redhair & blue eyes
will not rank among your kennings.

And if they do, you will lie to her, as you lied to me,

and I will no longer know the difference.

Watching the Leafs' latest streak, I am aware of a new impotence.

Once, I could stare at them and ensure they would fail, at that
precise second,

Hoglund would tear his rotator cuff, Sundin would
miss a penalty shot while the goalie ordered a foot-long in the stands.

I feel I must stop this and I am determined that they fall in the
playoffs until you die,

vowing that next year will be better, that a sudden parity of ice
and calls and luck will occur,

and you will plan to walk to Yonge Street, as you always threatened,
with a bullhorn and flag.

I am telling you that this will never happen; in telling you so,
I acknowledge that your dreams still plague me;

that I have an investment in them that I am hesitant to relinquish.

I was thinking of razoring your words from a card,
and pasting it here,

and realized I have none of them.

They all seem like mush to me, now, and then—

After I left on a trip while you were seeing the astrologer,
you slipped a letter in my bag.

It said that every time I left, you felt yourself slipping into a familiar
sadness, mitigated only by the thought of my return,

my skin, my eyes, something anatomical.

This would be the only card I remembered, for its audacity.

Among my socks and slips, these words.

Rattling before a strike I could not perceive: we were dead to each other,
and there is another felony there,

that involves indignity, the dumb aspect of a body, drained of its senses.

I wonder what it is to lie, the way you do. If it is like a child's story about
living on one's ceiling, or mingling among people who stand on their heads.

If it is constant, it is almost faultless.
That parable about the lying man and the honest man, giving directions.

In their two answers resides a precise certainty.

If I asked you what you ate, you would say tomato, not cheese;
if it was hot outside, you would recommend I wear a parka.

You brooded over *The Crow.* In it, the villainess says,
apropos of nothing, I like the pretty lies.

I only asked that you never bore me. But you did, by lying like a backwards
actuary or accountant,

spending your days crunching life, its monotony and excess,
into indistinct columns.

Ledgerly lies, that reflected your need to organize your life
erroneously,

like a housewife who irons towels, who mashes her husband's clothes
into the hamper,

without smelling them, for perfume, for sweat, for blood.

Stumping past one of the little galleries
that have appeared like a row of sutures on this ailing street—

the east wall is an urchin of balloons; in the window a neon sign:

Sigh
Cry
Almost
Die.

The last word blinks, irresolutely.

An old man rides by, a radio strapped to his bike playing swanky
French music,

I see stickers lined in rows on a tree, HI MY NAME IS—

Your name is there, in jagged cursive,
smudged, but legible

as some declining logic, a lyric about outlaws, about you:

C'était un gars loyal
Honnête et droit
Il faut croire

Que c'est la société
Qui m'a définitivement abîmé

Today at Wal-Mart—my arms filled with manicure scissors,
a can-opener, pliers, everything that has fallen apart

in the last week or so,

my friend mentioned seeing you,

the week we broke up, with your girlfriend.

She was dark and sultry, she said. A writer, and a good one.

She has met you both at a reading: this was not your girlfriend,
or your lover.

I know this, felt that she was referring to the Reformation as the Jazz Age:

I am tired of possessing a surfeit of information.

The brunette was yet another of my suspects, and she is nothing to me now.

She is nothing but the weight in my arms, righting an incorrigible history
of what is ruined; what will accede again,

as time passes, like the junk on the rubber beltway
that advances, rotates back.

There were too many letters to absorb, yet virtually every female
correspondent said the same thing, initially:

I know she does not like me, that she has a problem with me.

I did not know any of them.

I do admire your lies, at times like this: what had you said?

She is a large beetle, forever waving her feelers, drawing
inferences from thin air.

Indefensible claims: She throws rotting apples at me!

Kafka's diaries are surprisingly optimistic. He looks to the next
day. Slander is not interesting to him,

his wounds are self-inflicted.

Holing up in Ville D'Anjou for days, green
with stomach flu,

we crawled over each other, retching,
lay stiffly at either side of the single bed.

The day it abated, we walked with my grandfather
through the town,

stopped at my elementary school,
the park across the street,

across the rink where I slid and righted
myself, arms stretched,

my coat blown into a black bell.

This is the only picture you kept of me—

I wonder what you saw in it,
carelessness, or recovery.

How we were divided,
that we were capable of this.

You were afraid of flying; I was of no assistance.

I would shake you and point to the wing, insisting
it was in flames,

or had just snapped at the seams.

That I had seen the pilot drinking from a flask;
that "turbulence" is a well-known euphemism for "crash."

It was the take-offs you hated, and after that, me.

Habitually deafened, I yell at everything from the in-flight
feature to the same kid who kicks my seat, every time.

When I was bored, I pretended you were a dog,
and would ask,

What's the matter, boy? You hear something?
when you expressed agitation.

I always wondered why you dreaded the best part—

the sky should not support such suspension,
you knew this,

and resisted the extravagance of this lie.

Your new book is out. I look up the details online,
see you are as heavy as me,

your eyes, unlit, are two losenges.

He looks like he has been eating well, a casual friend said.
The comment moving like fork tines through pastry.

I let you feed yourself; your hipbones were like metal brackets.

I have solidified like a pudding.

This heavy armature a rejection of love and its remains.

If you saw me, this is all you would see: we are at the Seaquarium,
watching fish puff to ten times their size,

in seizures of dread and bravura.

We cross hands on the glass, passing by; you may pass by me
this way,

taking me in, moving forward. Towards the fins and spines of creatures
who signal without effort,

whose danger is blunt and certain; who cut the surface carelessly,
without reprisal.

Everyone ignored your grandmother; she was deaf and given to speculation.

Her neighbour was an assassin; her husband's son was roaming the
basement with a diagram and burlap bag.

She had been a seamstress, as delicate as a seam in silk.

The last time I saw her, I sat with her for hours
as you and your brother blasted CNN.

Osama bin Laden speaking from the mouth of a cave;
your mother making some kind of wurst, upstairs.

I hate war, she said. She said it a few times, and I nodded,
unable to touch her,

or see in her the girl who left Germany,
without her husband,

whose horrors seemed fair enough to me.

A file of soldiers she would never see. Among them,
her first marriage,

as cold as a fossil, hearing less than her,

the call of the sirens, a surrender she cannot imagine
as anything other than treachery, and theft.

My uncle is asked about his favourite sound: a key in the door, he says.

And I hear the deadbolt retracting, the hinges parting,
metal sliding on a ring.

You came home each night, fraught and determined, hefting cat litter,
or noodles, any of my requests:

cherry soda, a book about napalm, a roll of twine.

Crashing colanders, our one black-bellied pot: I would pretend I didn't hear you,
because you were all that I heard:

how your entrances and exits enclosed my life,

the small sandwiches I craved: I pooled like butter,
and kept this from you.

Other things I never said,

You are an essence, that is not sound. Coming home,
or leaving,

I leaned towards you, sighing.

I lean towards this. Some time, when my life ended and began.

You took me to Ontario Place, out of the blue.

Indulged my appetite for candy floss and corndogs,
rifle games and haunted houses.

You, who distrusted everything from planes to Spinning Teacups,
bought us tickets for a combination horror and log ride,

and as we flew past menacing bears, blinded by the spray,
as we took a few curves that genuinely frightened me, you smiled

and I was happy. Clearer is the sense of lining up with you,
with a hundred others, beside a trench of agates and amethyst,

waiting for you to give up, chicken out, whatever.

You breezed through the poke of the line and the children fished for stones
and the ride fell and rose.

I never knew why you took me, what had changed.

I am still happy, soaked and somehow small,
holding onto you, to the sides of the hollowed tree

that could have carried us to Hell, for all I care,
for all I cared.

Early on, my venal landlord stopped heating the
building, and eventually I could not leave the bed.

I was younger then and this kind of thing seemed inevitable.

I called everyone I knew, counted the blankets and listed them,
fortified myself, and froze.

You came over immediately with two space heaters.
Suddenly the room was warm, the hall; I was warm.

I admired your ingenuity, in this fix,

and this would always stay with me.

The idea that you could repair things that I was willing to discard;

that you, and your little apparatuses glowed,
saving me,

pole star, flash-fire.

How kind you were—this still humbles, and dazzles me.

I am thinking of the small fire on her fourth finger,
how it takes in the rooting light like a poke.

Feeling her tremble in the wake of your vows, that
you have become someone new,

for the love of her, in the interest of opportunity.

The vegetables that implode each week, before I replace them:
regardless of their firmness or slime,

the roots are complicated, and fixed.

Her hand reaches out, and seizes you. Drawing fractures
through your hair,

clawing the plain division, the way stars fall, as though
breaking the night.

Now and then, I imagined your death while you slept. I would
plan the funeral, an occasion on which I would behave deplorably,

and then cry until I woke you.

You would fling your arm over, and whisper some
blandishment or another, until I could sleep.

We looked like two hands on deck,
divided and bound in duty,

occasionally crossing paths, when greater forces conspired,
asking us to consider the peril

that entwined and isolated us.

I feel your arm now as I felt it then, as I felt what it might be like
if you were dead.

It felt like this. I feel this way.

You used to make a pasta dinner we named after you:
Fusilli noodles and beef jerky, Kraft Parmesan.

For the last two years, we balanced the bowls on our lap
and watched movies,

the dog sitting on your shoulder, eating off your fork.

Frank was another present: you had so few friends.

I came across him in a pet store, fighting a gang of Pomeranians
for a toy.

He had a herniated umbilicus, ingrown fangs, and was riddled
with worms.

When I held him he cried, and draped himself across me like a sash.

I knocked at your door and held him towards you.

You were outraged: You got him for yourself, you said.

And, melting, you stuck with him a year, mad for, mad about.

You would visit him after you left and cry, I love you I love you I love you.

This dog whines and kicks at me for hogging the blankets;
he is allergic to wool and MSG,

he likes to be walked in blizzards; will not pass a living creature without a fight.

I learned all this when you gave him up, and this is what I needed to learn.

That all of my love does not amount to a walk by a hydrant.

When he burrowed into the middle of the bed at night, you said,
He is something between us. And he is something between us.

In his sleep and yours, the objects move so quickly they blur. Your legs move, in pursuit,

and the space narrows and disappears.

I was the lonely one. He was mine, all along.

You married her.

Swearing up and down, tricked up in a shabby suit.

I consider her swaying by the hotel door, tears in her eyes.
You, gathering her close, and telling her, I will never leave you.

Having sworn this before God,

having realized, long ago, that mercy disregards the pulp of your lies;
that it extends its own arms to you,

that it will carry you forward, past each of us, the sum of your errors
that stack up like tissues,

what you extend in love, promises whole as mercury,
that break

into infinite replicas—her spine meeting matter, mine.

In your last florid letter, you said that you would, on occasion,
turn onto my street, where we had lived,

stand still before revolving home.

Your writing: boxes of black narcissi,
mink lashes.

What you forgot, what I would not remember for at least
a year,

that she lived there too, in that awful rectangle I paced
like a prison yard,

measuring its perimeter in inches.

I passed her once, as she sorted through her mail,
cool, indifferent.

Turned the corner and cried for what it cost,
to move along like a streak of chalk,

an ant carrying its entire weight back
to the colony, the furrow in the sand you slipped from—

from a distance there are hills and hills,
each indistinguishable,

one trembles with a new familiarity, another, uncovered,
is crushed:

your writing, a column,
black jaws opening like scissors.

Something like authenticity yields,
and devises the raid.

I ask my hairdresser about her break-up,
reported to me by my sister on Valentine's Day:

a farrago of screaming and pitched face gels.

She nods at her fiancé who is mixing dye behind her,
smiles.

Cold feet.

I mention that you left me and she looks uncomfortable:
I realize later I have been saying this for over two years.

I feel like a cutter, slicing over white scars;
the man who cuts my lawn, who cannot stop telling me

how he sold flowers on Mother's Day, how his parcel of
counterfeit twenties was seized at the end of the night.

They're all in on it, the banks, the robbers. I hear you Bob,
I always say, it's hard.

It's hard to relinquish this story—it has come to define me
as an entire dynasty, as its remnants,

a crate of fragile vases, dry and displaced.

When I dream of you, I am not dreaming of you.

I am dreaming of fear, and it is compelling. It fixes me
somewhere, not here,

where betrayal and loss smoulder, and I falter
among the sparks,

that mutate in their burning,
taking shape.

You had been gone a year, and I called you.

Don't leave me, I said.

You were rational, not unkind. I left you a long time ago, you said.

It is time that confuses me, how it combines its progress,
without perforations or borders.

Like a drawing executed in thirds, that unfolds to reveal a whole.

You appear to occupy vacancies that no longer exist.

Frank recently cried after a man who looked like you,
in passing.

I sympathize, as I continue to sleep on one side of the bed.

I do not want you back, but my life, your part in its unspoken promises—
I want that, what was undone, what was never made.

I mistake it for your lolling head, your coiled feet, the six mouths of your bureau,
each of them stuffed with whatever it was

that kept you beside me,

whatever compelled you to open and then close your displeasure; to return
it to its precarious vault,

to return to me.

Anger to memory is arson, accelerated
in varying degrees.

There is our apartment, its exposed wires
and loose sockets;

a dryer filled with lint, its three-prong cord
bisecting a puddle;

a gas oven, seeping slowly; extensions snaking into
a blackened outlet.

The air wavers, extending feelers, when I return,
and dictate to myself that I remember

what it was, how I apprehended each danger.

He never stayed with me, your friend tells me. He was in a hotel
with his co-workers, her.

I will be travelling a lot with her, you tell me. I'll stay, if you
do not complain.

I thought it was her, someone says.

I am still shocked. It has been so long, and my anger remains latent,
the current that shot through each split connection
and held, as if mindful of my worst terror.

Sparking elsewhere: we are standing on our porch, speaking quietly.

She passes by and holds up two mittened hands, they open and close,
the gesture blinding me.

I was electrocuted once. Somewhere between the wet light
and the floor, my bones inverted.

Shaking through it, I drew inward, preparing myself.

For a greater charge: her hands snapped like tongs and caught me:
I knew something terrible.

What was not visible, what surged beyond us,
knitting itself into disaster, over time.

You could have revealed everything: how you would borrow my
cellphone and clear its call records,

make bizarre trips explained as other odious errands, for me,

where you were, what you looked at—

thrown it up, as if showing me how to play fifty-two pickup.

You just nodded, and turned in.

Woke me up, the same way, with coffee. You don't love me anymore,
I cried, and the sound pushed you away,

backwards, out the door, towards the roll of tape and muffled apologies,
more tactful lies.

I waited for you to tell, and did not know what was waiting, all that time,
what is waiting: I have never collected.

Nailed your kneecaps to the floor, got down and assembled each card.

Four suits, radiant with meaning: what formalities we extended to each other,
how easily you called my hand.

Raking the contents of your closet into bags and boxes.

It is the morning of my birthday, my second without you.

Nothing has changed, you are nothing to me.

You are the line in my palm I thought would be an accident:
it breaks into an isosceles triangle, and resumes.

My life will be calculated this way—what transpired before and after
the crash,

crowns wedged on broken teeth, a streak of scar tissue,
how one learns to feel the imminence of rain.

You would look through windows, as if plotting this disaster.

How speed and circumstance converge in sound and light.

The moon was inclined to rest against you, madly in love.
Sighs escaped you, rushing sweetly—

I would not have noticed, noticing now
how I rotate backwards, ushering you back.

To dispel you: the warp in the mattress I fall into,
some sudden breezes,

sighing me back to sleep.

I hear things about you, largely neutral,
if mystifying in the details,

possibly, a glass of beer; the new shape of your face;
a small vulgarity involving faulty plumbing.

I am tempted, at times, to challenge the decisions you have made,
their banality and grandeur—

a cramped apartment slanting into a diamond, two.

To circle you like a felon,
a poem that reaches back like a rake, turning over vines,

orange blossoms, round petals as luxurious as skin.

I will pause at times, hefting tomatoes or apricots,
and wish I had joined you in this, other excursions.
That I had seen you, growing stronger,

passing me over, too hard, too ripe, too bruised—

I wish I could have seen you bagging garlic,
watched you open them, razor each clove.

That I had never waited for the end, for what I loved,
the warm plate, its tendrils of steam,

your body, beside me, imperfect, sublime,
complaining the night,

in sudden jackknives, blurred complaints.

Once or twice the moon aggressed the window.

Your beauty glared and I missed you,

I miss you, what you continue to radiate,
like a vein of gold.

Fugitive evidence, that ruins me,
and leads me forward,

also shining, the spikes of a sunflower, visible through a hurricane fence,

the edge of light, sealing us together,
before we scattered, taking sides.

You told me you were having a baby,
with such tenderness, I felt myself being arranged around your words.

I had been thinking, these last few days, about how we began,
about your love

that I never trusted. It was electrical, poured from you
in a way that made me look for cover.

I did not want or deserve it, and as I see it now, forging covenants,
making life,

I am asking you to walk into the rain with me; you are too prudent.

I am standing in the rain, alone, and the skies swell and calm—

And I ask you anyway, why you did not choose me.

My life has changed, you say.

I tell you the same thing, abbreviating each word with tears.

Suddenly it has ended. You can't hurt me anymore, I think.

I think of the umbilicus as a flare of lightning, how it rolls you two, three,
together,

how long I have looked through my window, trying to beguile its every streak,
to dispel what I see and feel,

also seeing that it is a covenant that excludes me.

I am shaking off the last of the rain that falls for you, that beats against me,
the careless lightning asserting its distance, its ability to strike.

Certain objects: dead babies, unborn babies, breathless, unwanted,
an absence of hope: the idea that it can erase you like a chalk mark,

the chalk marks I have seen,

scrawling out hearts. Names joined with crosses, small coffins, a horrible wail, love,

expended in violence, mutable convictions,
other intangibles.

Arctic with shock, I told you everything.

There are always men, I said. Other distractions.

I saw a rat in the yard, not a rat exactly: thread-tailed, still,
a baby werewolf.

There is a werewolf in the yard, I told my brother,
described it.

He told me it was a possum, reminded me that they play dead.

I consider how my mind fires like a race-car, from 0 to 90:
what laws are broken, consequently.

Speeding through this block of time, every turn and wreck an irritant,
from start to finish.

Everything is the same, however dreadful:

the moon rises like a flush of burning metal, exposing the distance
between what I know to be true

and my desperation to desert it.

I had stopped writing about you, early on. I was afraid you would
read the diaries, take offense.

The last entry is about the tattoo, this time I notice your body
is a cemetery, that each addition marks someone dead.

The red flag that was the window where you found a friend,
decomposing in the half-light,

obscure poets, Blake's inept phrasing of God.

My name in a heart, transplanted. How you punished yourself,
making room.

Your mother must have made lederhosen by now,
pinafores, wool stockings;

she is freezing small portions of sauerkraut,
proofing the electricals,

telling you again, a few glasses in, how your brother was so
sickly she camped at the foot of his crib.

That when you were born you let loose
"an enormous bowel movement," startling the doctor.

I have nodded at the same stories,
marvelling at what little they reveal to her

about the fiercest of her passions.

Her modest collection of lifelike ceramic dolls.

One, a boy in a blue jumper, screws up his face
as a caterpillar negotiates his fat arm.

I would have crawled, if I had to, to change.

Today, I saw a Piglet doll upended on the street,
one of the names I called you then,

that luxuriates in the first diary: I read it and see myself growing heavy
with your beauty, your persistence.

A photograph slips out, your long, coiled hair,
limpid eyes also,

your skin breathing plums, cherries, the stain of your lips.

I am desperate, you said, crying. I noted this, other tears,
with amusement and resolve.

It was wrong, and inexorable. I was afraid of you, and still,
I was tired of resisting,

such voluptuous admissions, your adamance.

The kind of bird that is allowed to fly around the house.

This bird retreats to its perch, convincing itself that night falls in a length
of velvet—

your hands enfolding me, make a shell, and there is some ruffling,
one or two cries, as the darkness falls.

When you called, you were washing dishes. I could hear birds
screeching: there are a lot of trees here, you said.

I thought this marriage was an error in judgement, I said.

You told me it was forever. As if you had all the time in the world.

I can't have children, I said. You said you were sorry,
sorry also to hear me this way.
When I asked you why, you said it just happened.

Nothing happens: branches extend themselves, the birds
start ferrying twigs back and forth.

The tree in my yard expels eggs every spring. I pick the pale blue
shards from the yellow pulp.

I tell you that I love you, and I do.

You shook me off, reaching past, but I still return.

Empty and smudged, the bowl you push into the water,
easing out its remains, drying it until it squeaks.

The window in front of you glows, obscuring you
from me,

the sun glances, and happens to glance, on the wet,
curved surfaces you place in rows,

another surface: her body pushing forward like a spoon,
slotting itself into your back.

I want to finish this, to break the jar, to scale this obstacle,
no matter what I feel,

that you killed me, that I have experienced everything since
like something starving, hardly sentient.

That I want to return to your unmade bed, and watch the moon
invent you, latching us together.

Or tell you, No. This will end badly, I am capable of being alone.

I am capable of being alone, but it has deformed me.

I have loved life better because of this—
I would have died for you, I said. And have, in parts.

You would have continued to visit me, and I refused, bored,
I thought.

Three days before you left me, I went to the hospital. The doctor
was cold and abrupt.

I phoned you and cried, you said, Come home. It's all right, come home.

This is what I missed, what is missing.

The lies were incidental. I rushed back, and you were there,
where you always were.

Half-listening, distracted.

Gesturing anyway, to places I could lean: your chest, inside the spaces
you made for me: your arms,

the violet and lilac walls, the side of the bed I have never relinquished.

Some times you would roll over and find me; your back consoling me.

My key moving in the lock alerted you, moving towards me as I pushed
the door back,

I would forget what brought me there; I cannot forget what it felt like,
that you asked, that I came home.

I thought you were over him? someone said, and I made up this
metaphor,

about an accident, the incongruence between who is at fault,
and the severity of the pain.

How some head injuries will always tell you about imminent rain,
how time assembles itself like a riptide between balanced waves;

the tracks of a wild animal, disappearing at the tree line;

the pattern of tire marks, a loss of density.

We are driving in a snowstorm, somewhere.
Glass roads, white nausea.

The gales shake the car and we are rigid
with fear, there are two images:

our hands, white contractions;
my coat pinwheeling as I fall out of the car.

We have arrived safely: the city looks like a loaf of bread;
you rush over and right me,

ploughing over, you made a culvert.

Every time I fall, I consider the relative safety of motion and stasis,
and imagine you and me stopping short at the end.

The last time you tried to say goodbye,
I printed the letter, and taped it in a diary

that reads like a dance card, box steps, fox-trots,
this tango: intricate and determined.

In the second paragraph, a rhyme—

I remember, Lynn, I remember too. Watching you at times you never knew.

Other plain elegies, admissions.

Reading this, I think of your lies as a paper lantern, paste diamonds,
frail vanities,

afraid of, offended by deliberate cruelty.

It is enough, knowing this.

I curled up and slept, or looked through windows too,
you looked at me, I never knew.

What I have forgotten—

something taking root, blind and insensible,
carried forward, and preserved.

This remains fluid, if bitter or piercing,
how I have been suspended, deformed myself, in love with you.

ACKNOWLEDGMENTS

I want to thank Leanne Delap, for her generous and careful first reading of this book, and offer her violets, *but violent, more violent.*

Adrienne Weiss, an early editor and true Belladonna.

Also, my family, Janet Stone, David McGimpsey, and James Crosbie for their faultless support, always.

Martha Sharpe, for her long-standing encouragement.

At Anansi: Ken, a writer, an editor to live up to. Sarah, Lynn, and Laura for their great kindness.

And particular thanks to Joanne Balles, Kevin Connolly, Gil Adamson, Esta Spalding, Stuart Ross — happily, my friends.

To Bruce McDonald, who chose the title, and, among *all my pretty ones*, the very inspiring Michael Turner, Dominic Patten, Jake Richler, James Pattyn, Nick Mount, Liz Renzetti, Sherwin Tjia, William New, and Rani Rivera.

Some of these poems were published in *Taddle Creek*, *The Walrus* and *Sid & Shirley.*

Others are indebted to Antonin Artaud, Bob Dylan, Ernest Hemingway, Elizabeth Bishop, Hole, Jacqueline Susann, John Donne, Leonard Cohen, Louis Jordan, Nirvana, Serge Gainsbourg, Sylvia Plath, Ted Hughes, and a *Toronto Life* rejection letter.

Still others, and all, are, at heart, dedicated to the one I loved.

AUTHOR PHOTO: JAMES PATTYN

ABOUT THE AUTHOR

Lynn Crosbie is a cultural critic and the author of four books of poetry: *Miss Pamela's Mercy*, *VillainElle*, *Pearl* (a finalist for the Pat Lowther Award), and a collection of new and selected work, *Queen Rat*. She is also the author of the controversial book *Paul's Case*, and is the editor of *The Girl Wants To* and *Click*. Lynn Crosbie has a PhD in English Literature, and teaches at the Ontario College of Art and Design, and the University of Toronto.